In Fredericksburg
The Past & Presence of an Old Virginia Town

In Fredericksburg
The Past & Presence of an Old Virginia Town

EDITED BY RONALD SHIBLEY WITH PHOTOGRAPHS BY TAYLOR LEWIS

Parson Weems Press

Text copyright 1984 by Ronald E. Shibley
Photographs copyright 1984 by Taylor Lewis

All rights reserved, including the right to reproduce this book or any portions thereof in any form.
Published by the Parson Weems Press, Fredericksburg, Virginia

Produced and Designed by Cognoscenti

INTRODUCTION

In eighteenth and nineteenth century Virginia the mostly rural countryside was dotted with large and small towns which served as centers of political, social, cultural and economic life. Men and women and their families spent most of their lives living and working in or near the towns of old Virginia. People living in the countryside depended heavily upon the merchants of the nearest town to provide goods and services. "Going to town" was a major social event for many Virginia families well into the twentieth century.

Most of Virginia's oldest towns have now disappeared, lost forever in the rapid growth of urban and suburban communities. But the concept of town life remains very much alive in Fredericksburg, one of Virginia's oldest municipalities. Chartered in 1728, Fredericksburg has retained its unique identity and way of life. In the historic district and in neighborhoods near the old downtown, private residences from three centuries exist side by side with commercial businesses, museum houses, religious buildings, governmental offices and public parks.

Many of Fredericksburg's buildings are still used for their original purpose, some by descendants of their original owners. Other houses have been adapted for contemporary use. This large number of old buildings in an attractive physical setting has helped the town preserve its identity. No bedroom community of anonymous residents, Fredericksburg has a lively political and social life. Townspeople greet each other on the street and—often to the amazement of many visitors—also speak to strangers. An openness to outside influence has made it possible for newcomers to assimilate into the old community. Many have become more attached to the city's traditional values than some long-time residents.

IN FREDERICKSBURG: THE PAST AND PRESENCE OF AN OLD VIRGINIA TOWN captures the special quality of life, of history, or architecture and of environment which make Fredericksburg unique. A living community with a rich architectural and historical heritage, Fredericksburg exhibits a continuing sense of time and place. This book represents in photographs, like those of Matthew Brady and Frances Benjamin Johnston did years ago, the beauty, charm and grace of "Virginia's most historic town."

From its beginning in 1728 as a hinterlands town on the western edge of British America, Fredericksburg served as a center of life for the people of the Rappahannock River watershed. The neighboring counties of Stafford and Spotsylvania had no principal towns, except Falmouth, a mile up the Rappahannock River on the river's east bank. It was a crossroads town of taverns, lodgings, commerce and shipping. The main overland transportation routes, first the carriage road and then the railroad, ran through Fredericksburg. People came from as far west as Culpeper, Orange and Fauquier counties to buy supplies, to transact their legal and political affairs, and for social and cultural activities.

The early population of the town numbered in the hundreds, clustered in a small, 50-acre area along the west bank of the river. Originally laid out in a grid pattern with wide streets, each named after British royalty, and 64 equal-sized lots, plus two lots for a church and a market, the city outgrew its boundaries quickly. In 1759, the physical size was tripled by taking in an area west to the present site of Winchester Street.

Additional changes were made in 1851–52, when the town's size was tripled again by moving the boundary westward to the present location of Sunken Road. Three times in the mid-twentieth century, in 1940, 1951, and 1955, largely rural areas were taken into the city. In 1984 Fredericksburg grew to its present size, 10.5 square miles with 18,500 residents, by annexation of a large area of Spotsylvania County west of the city. The annexation left Fredericksburg with over seven miles of riverfront land along the scenic Rappahannock. Most of this land along the river is still undeveloped, adding significantly to the almost rural look of the town.

The site for the town was selected owing to its location just below the fall line of the Rappahannock, the point at which the river ceases to be tidal. The oldest section, the historic district, is located on a sloping site on the plains above the river's west bank. The low hills and steep slopes, formed by several small streams, which rose above the old town are now within the city. Occupied mostly by Mary Washington College and the battlefields of the National Park Service, these hills were the site of gun emplacements and troop trenches during the terribly bloody Battle of Fredericksburg in December 1862. West of the hill line the countryside is flatter but still includes deep ravines and heavily wooded lots.

The rolling, hilly countryside of the Fredericksburg area presents a wide variety of topography, giving the town and environs the appearance of a small village. The river forms the northern and eastern boundary of the city. One of the last unpolluted tidal rivers in Virginia, the Rappahannock offers some of the most beautiful scenery in the town. From the white water rapids above the town at its westernmost border, near an historic river crossing, the river drops in elevation over seventy feet in the approximately five miles to the tidal line at Falmouth.

The river, the source of the town's being, provided power for eighteenth and nineteenth century mills, and, in our century, for electric power. After every heavy rainfall muddy raging torrents cascade down from upriver, carrying the top soil from upland counties. On most days the river is placid and flat, its water surface looking almost black, as it flows slowly over the ancient riverbed rocks, some shaped by Indians into fish traps dating to Paleolithic times. The Rappahannock has become a popular recreational site for activities ranging from fishing, swimming, picnicing to canoeing and "tubing," the economical and exciting way to ride downriver through the rapids on an old inner tube. In the spring the riverbank is crowded with fishermen seeking the herring and shad which come here each year to spawn.

From Falmouth southeastward the river is tidal. Wide tidal flats appear at some points during low tide. Where sailing ships once brought cargoes into the docks and warehouses and carried away agricultural and industrial products, the river is now mostly park land, protected now from future development. The old warehouse related to riverborne commerce are gone, except the Old Stone Warehouse on Sophia Street. The days of sailing declined with the coming of the railroad and after the river began to fill with the rich topsoil washed down from the agricultural lands of Orange, Culpeper and Fauquier counties. The last riverborne cargo is limited at present to the oil barges which come to the small terminal at the extreme southeastern end of the town.

Much change has come to Fredericksburg since World War II. Before the war the town had not changed very much in the previous half-century. Still very dependent upon the agricultural activities of adjacent counties and a few small industries, it was still a crossroads village offering services and goods to a wide area of central Virginia. The war brought new people and new businesses, yet Fredericksburg never lost its special character. Most of the city is occupied by single family homes, small apartment buildings and townhouses. The tree-lined streets of the older sections are distinctively different from the scattered developments around the towns edges.

For most of the last 200 years the downtown commercial and business district served as the retail center for the whole Fredericksburg area. The shopping centers of the 1960s and 1970s changed all that. No longer the only retail and social center in the area, Fredericksburg has adjusted to the change and the growth of the area. The historic district downtown has been rejuvenated through private investment in renovation and restoration. The municipal government added brick sidewalks, period style lamps and other amenities. A new park on the river is now being built. The development of small shops, restaurants, renovated apartments and service businesses has returned the town to its original concept. Now once again a very special trading center with a unique and distinctive architectural and historical appeal, the historic district is becoming a successful example of contemporary urban revitalization.

In the years ahead even more change will come to the old town. With their long history of growth and adaptation to change, the residents of Fredericksburg will surely do their best to retain their historic special identity for the benefit of future generations.

RONALD E. SHIBLEY

Grave of John Coalter, who died at Chatham, St. George's Church cemetery.

1 **Chatham**—West Lawn

From the handsome brick manor house at Chatham the view of the town is panoramic. Built in 1765 on a commanding bluff on the north bank of the river opposite Fredericksburg, Chatham was the home of William Fitzhugh, grandfather of Robert E. Lee.

George Washington, the Marquis de Lafayette, Walt Whitman and Clara Barton were among the prominent visitors. Used as a command post by the Union forces during the Battle of Fredericksburg, Chatham is now a visitor center for the area battlefields maintained by the National Park Service.

2 Chatham—East Lawn

In Spring the east lawn at Chatham is fragrant with the scent of hundreds of roses in the mass planting seen here. Nearby are the recently restored greenhouses.

3 Vista from Chatham

The cupola of the Courthouse and the spires of St. Georges Episcopal and Fredericksburg Baptist churches still dominate the town's skyline as they did in December 1862 when the Union army's artillery fired upon Fredericksburg from the lawn in front of Chatham.

4 Chatham from the Town

In winter and early spring Chatham is visible through the trees from the town side of the Rappahannock.

5 The Rappahannock above Falmouth

The rolling green hills of the Rappahannock River valley and the rapids above the fall line at Falmouth are part of the view from Clearview, an eighteenth century home above the town of Falmouth. At right, in the background, is Belmont, the home of Gari Melchers.

6 Belmont Grounds and Melcher's Studio

Impressionist painter Gari Melcher resided here from 1916 until his death in 1932. The Melchers bought the property from the family of Joseph B. Ficklen, a manufacturer who had acquired the Belmont site in 1824. Ficklen's milling operation, the Bridgewater Mill, was across the Rappahannock at the fall line, in sight of the house.

Central Rappahannock Regional Library

7 A contemporary view of the William Street bridge, built 1939–1941. The circa 1910 photograph, "Fredericksburg from Stafford Heights," was first published in a calendar produced by Robert Kishpaugh, a local printer. Kishpaugh's interest in old Fredericksburg resulted in some of the best historical photographs of the town. The old bridge was called "Free Bridge," because it replaced an earlier toll bridge. The iron bridge was lost during the great flood of 1937.

9 A Gambrel-Roofed Colonial House

The streets of Fredericksburg are graced by a variety of architectural styles. There are only a few gambrel-roofed homes, a style preferred in the late eighteenth-century. An early twentieth century brick home and a nineteenth century frame dwelling are its neighbors in this photograph.

10 **George Street Entrance, National Bank**

Built about 1820, the bank building included an upstairs residence for the bank manager. This was the entrance to the family quarters. The leaded glass tracery over the door was restored in 1984, when other exterior repairs were made.

11 **Presbyterian Church Houses**

Three houses from the first half of the nineteenth century. They are owned by the Presbyterian Church of Fredericksburg and are being restored.

STATE HOUSE, FREDERICKSBURG, VA.

12 **Steeples and Towers on Princess Anne St.**

One of the Brady group of Civil War photographers captured a scene on this street in 1863 or 1864. The same three structures dominate the streetscape today. James Renwick, Jr. designed a Moorish-inspired courthouse which has been altered from the original plan. The mislabeled drawing, "State House, Fredericksburg, Va." reveals the original design, with parapet walls and without the cornice on the bell tower.

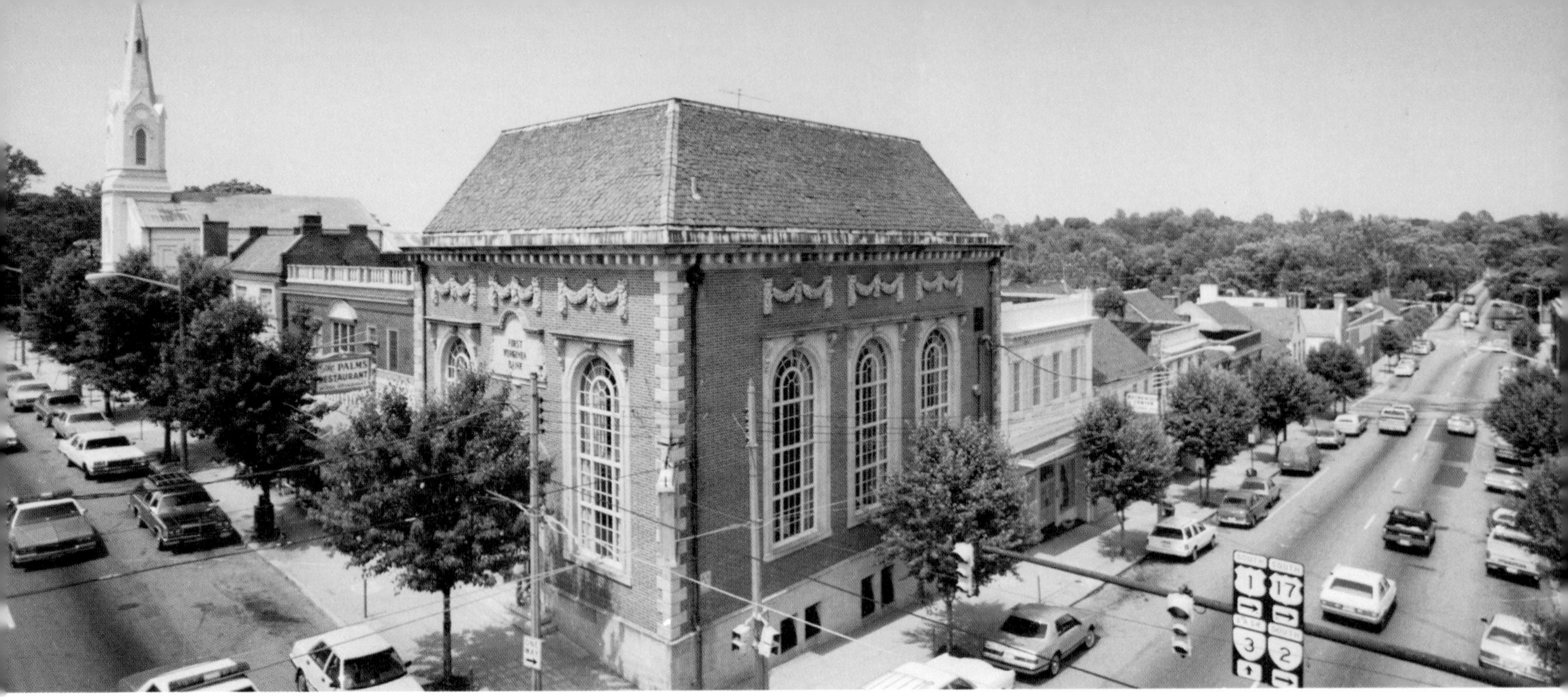
PALMS
RESTAURANT
1
17
3
2

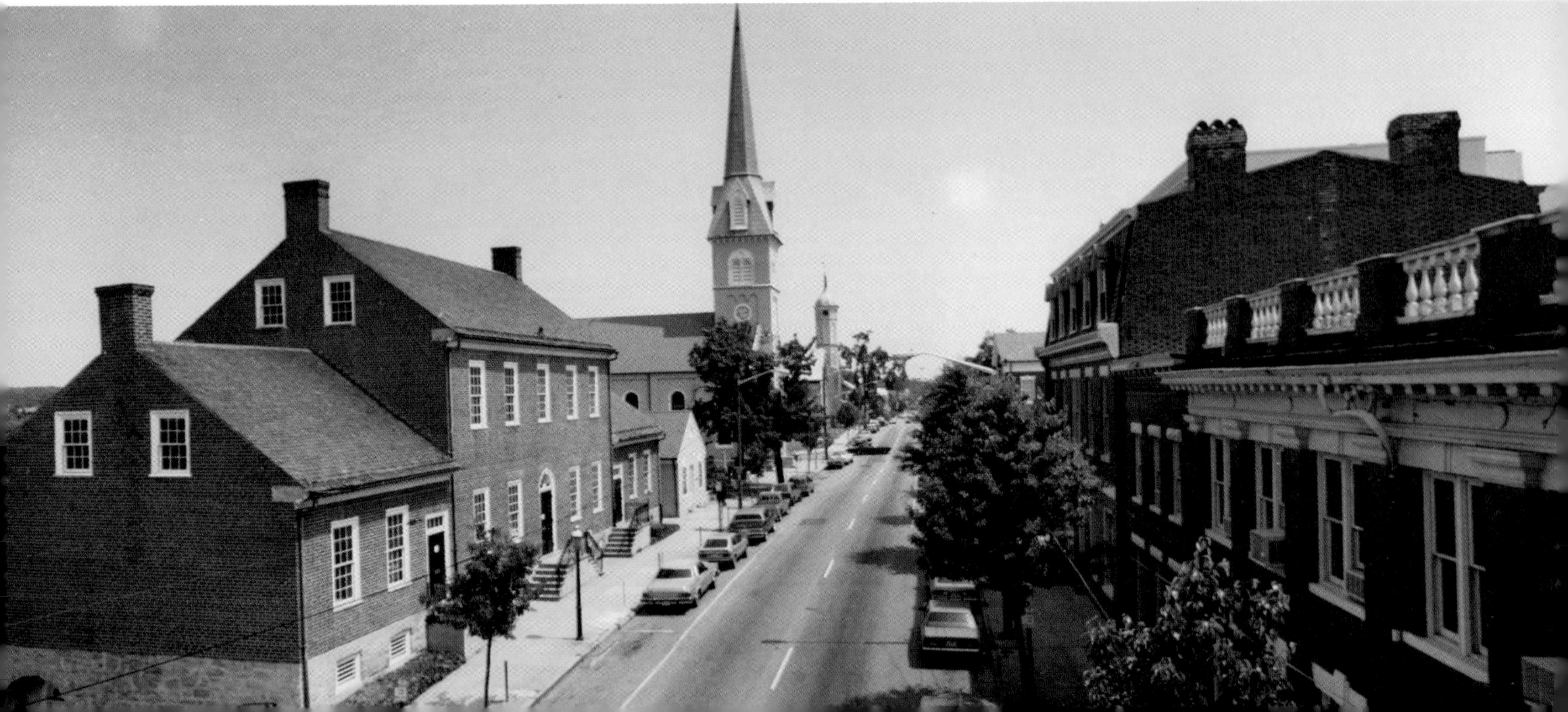

15 **Two Vistas of Princess Anne Street**

The Fredericksburg Baptist Church (1855), the old Planters National Bank (1928), old City Hall (1814), St. George's Episcopal Church (1849) and the Courthouse (1851) are still the most prominent features on Princess Anne Street. Their continued presence contributes significantly to the special sense of the enduring value of the past so evident along the streets of Fredericksburg.

16 **City Hall, 1927**

Photographed by Frances Benjamin Johnston, the first American architectural photographer of her sex.

17 **Ornamental Metal Work, Star Building, 1888**

The legend "Mesker Bros., St. Louis, Mo." appears elsewhere on the facade.

18 **The Victorian Influence**

In the second half of the last century the Victorian styles of commercial construction were the most popular. In the 1000 block of Caroline Street is the largest collection in the town. From the Queen Anne tower at left to the mansard roofs of the Second Empire buildings at center the tastes of another century are still reflected.

19 **Visitor Center**

The tourism information service provided by the City of Fredericksburg has its headquarters in this early nineteenth century row house on Caroline Street. Rehabilitation of the building in 1975 was one of the early steps taken to encourage the revival of the historic district.

20 The grand yet graceful arches of the Richmond, Fredericksburg and Potomac Railroad bridge (1925–1928) from the Stafford County bank of the river. This was one of the last poured concrete bridges in the United States.

Iron fence on George Street, c. 1830.

21 Charles Mortimer House

The town of Fredericksburg expanded eastward along the Rappahannock in the middle of the eighteenth century in the area now called lower Caroline Street. Among the first homes built was this fine brick dwelling house owned by Mayor Charles Mortimer, the town's first elected official. The street is still one of the most beautiful residential neighborhoods in the town.

22 The 1927 view of the Charles Mortimer House by Frances Benjamin Johnston.

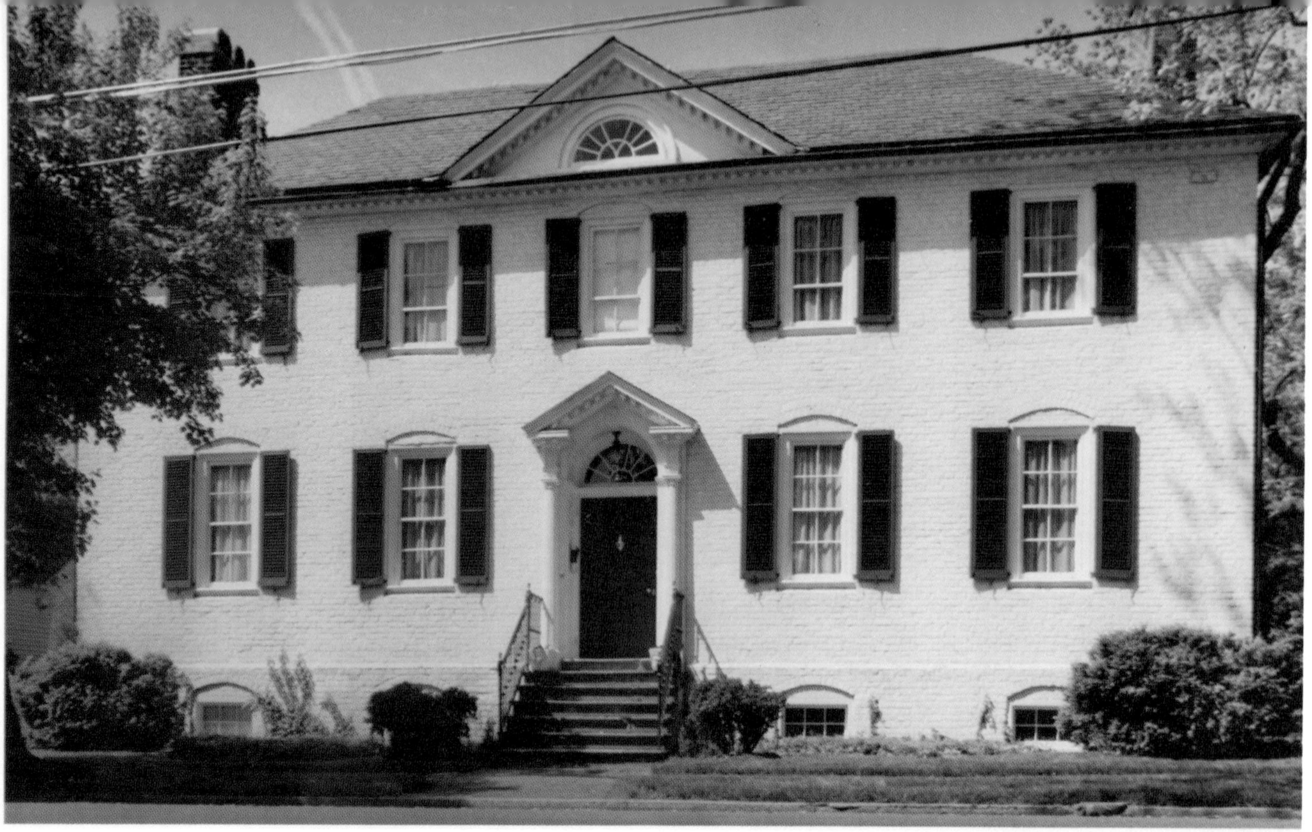

23 The restored Georgian entrance at the Matthew Fontaine Maury House

24

25

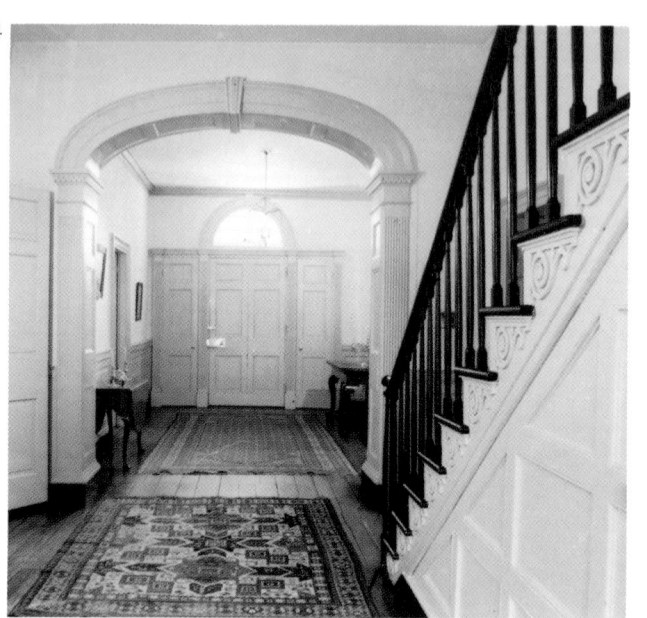

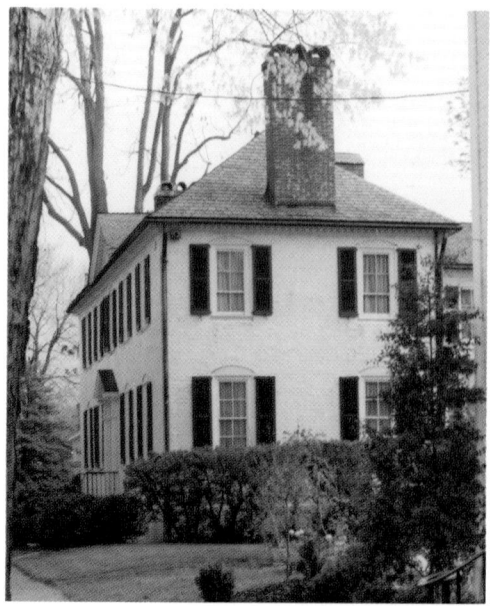

26

23 **Matthew Fontaine Maury House**

Once the home of Matthew Fontaine Maury, "The Pathfinder of the Seas," this eighteenth century brick house dates to the 1780s. It was among the first houses built on lower Caroline Street after the Revolutionary War.

24 Stair hall and entrance with fan light transom

25 North End, Maury House

26 The Drawing Room

28

27 **Matthew Fontaine Maury House**
The Dining Room with Chinese-inspired design on hand-painted wallpaper

28 Dining Room mantel with Chinese export porcelain and polished brass fireplace accessories

Tracery with arrows

Smithsonia, 1834

29 The 1770 House

A modest eighteenth century house on Princess Anne Street said to have been a carriage house for one of the larger residences on nearby Caroline Street.

30 Warehouses

The old brick warehouses near the City Dock were lost to demolition earlier this century. The land they occupied, south of the RF&P railroad bridge, is still vacant.

Library of Congress

31 City Dock Houses

Along lower Sophia Street at the old city dock, now the site of a municipal park, these two old houses appear to be on a rural county road. Just three blocks from the center of the town, they overlook the tidal area of the Rappahannock. The brick house, recently enlarged, is said to have been the residence of the keeper of the ferry to George Washington's farm across the river. The frame house is an eighteenth century cottage relocated from Charles Street in the early 1970s. The Toll-keepers house is also seen in the 1927 photograph.

Circular motif transom

Geometric tracery window

32 307 Caroline Street

Built before 1795 this frame house on lower Caroline Street has been modified several times to reflect popular architectural styles.

34 Greek Revival Town Houses

In the second quarter of the nineteenth century the Greek Revival style came to the town in the design for the new Presbyterian Church and in these five town houses on lower Caroline Street, opposite the Sentry Box. Four of the five have been restored. The accompanying Civil War photograph, probably taken in 1864, reveals the devastating effects of the war.

36 Carriage Drive

The brick carriage drive of the Charles Mortimer House overlook the Rappahannock, just a block away. The country look is deceiving, since the house is on Caroline Street in the historic district and close to the center of town.

National Park Service

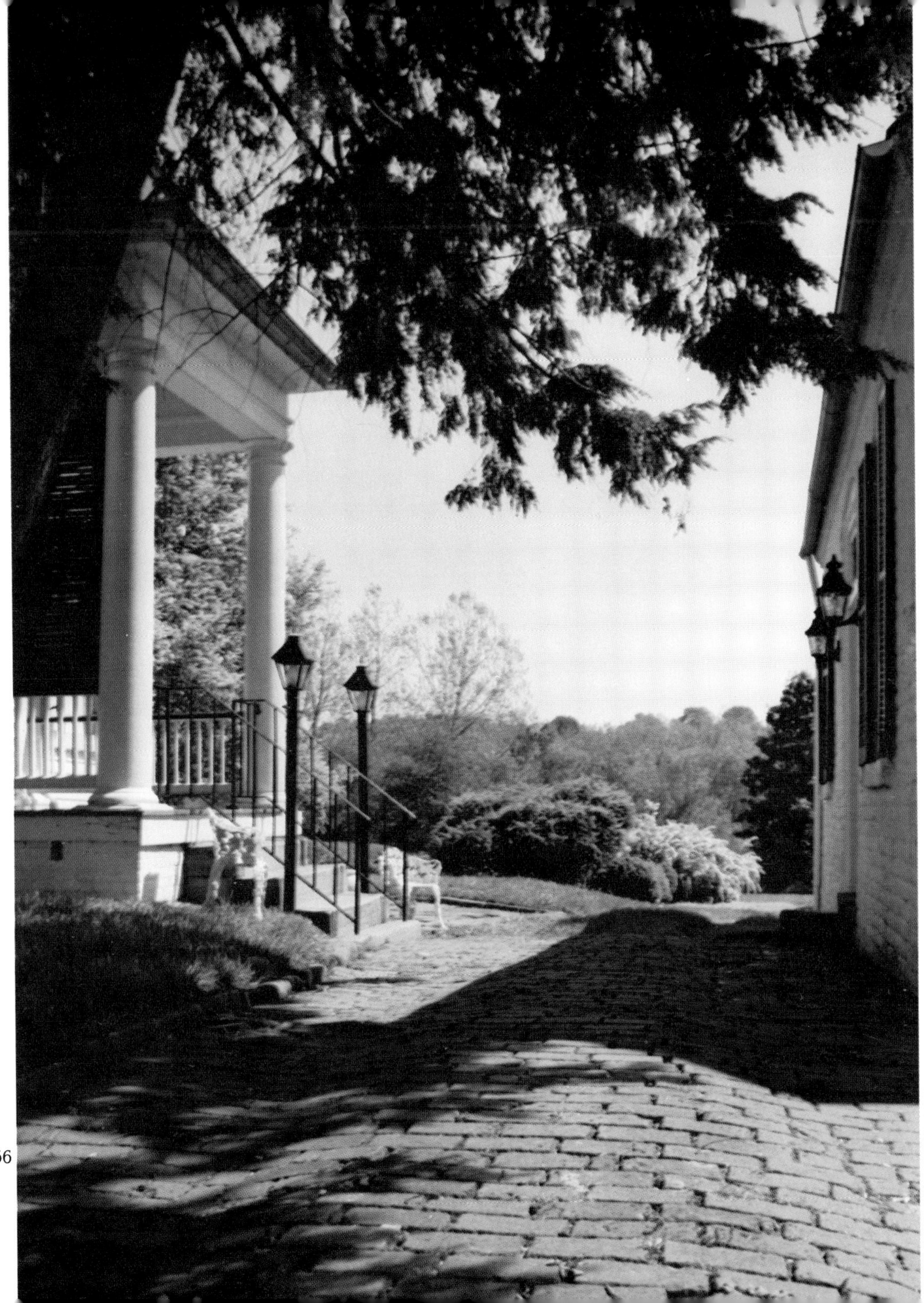

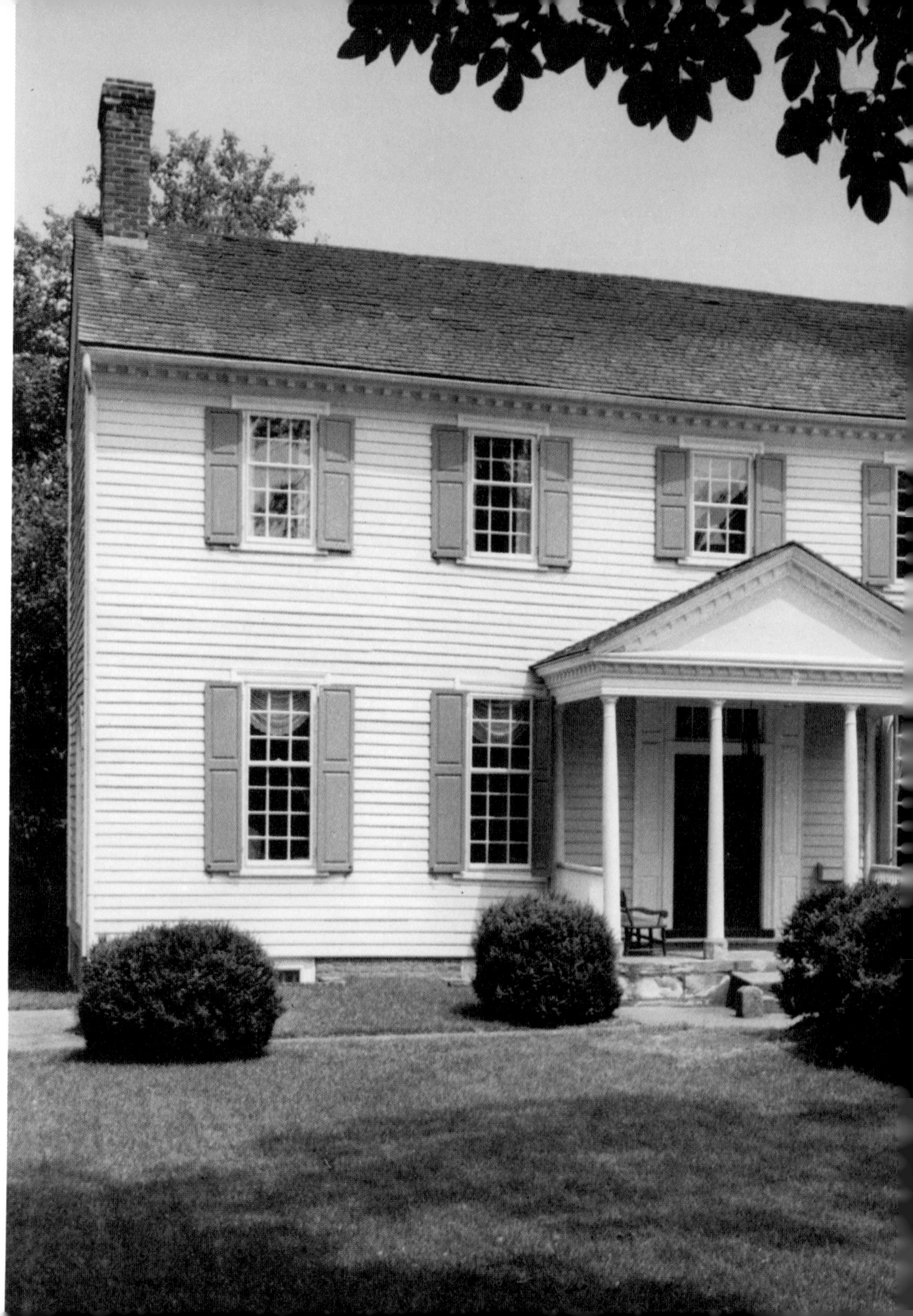

37 General Weedon's Sentry Box

One of several generals supplied by Fredericksburg to the Revolutionary army, George Weedon came home from the war and built this house on a river bluff on lower Caroline Street. On one of the largest privately owned lots in the town, the Sentry Box overlooks the Rappahannock on one side and the restored lower Caroline Street neighborhood on the other. Restoration of the Sentry Box helped start the movement toward the rebuilding of Fredericksburg's historic heritage.

38 Two Versions of Victoriana

Side by side on lower Caroline Street are these two Victorian homes.

39 Square-towered Victorian House, Lower Caroline St.

A square central tower is unusual in Fredericksburg. On lower Caroline Street the oldest houses are Georgian or Federal, yet this Italianate Victorian residence on a large lot blends well with its neighbors.

40 Old House, Old Boxwood

One of the Civil War photographs of Fredericksburg taken in 1862 or 1863 shows Union army nurses on the porch of a two-story frame house with four large brick chimneys. The site may have been this early 1800s residence on Caroline Street, now restored after a long period of decline. The boxwood garden dates to the early twentieth century.

40

41 Urban Revival

These nineteenth century houses, once dilapidated and almost abandoned, are being restored. The projection of the porch over the sidewalk gives the house an Italian look. Only one other house in the town has a similar porch.

42 Topiary boxwood garden, Princess Anne Street

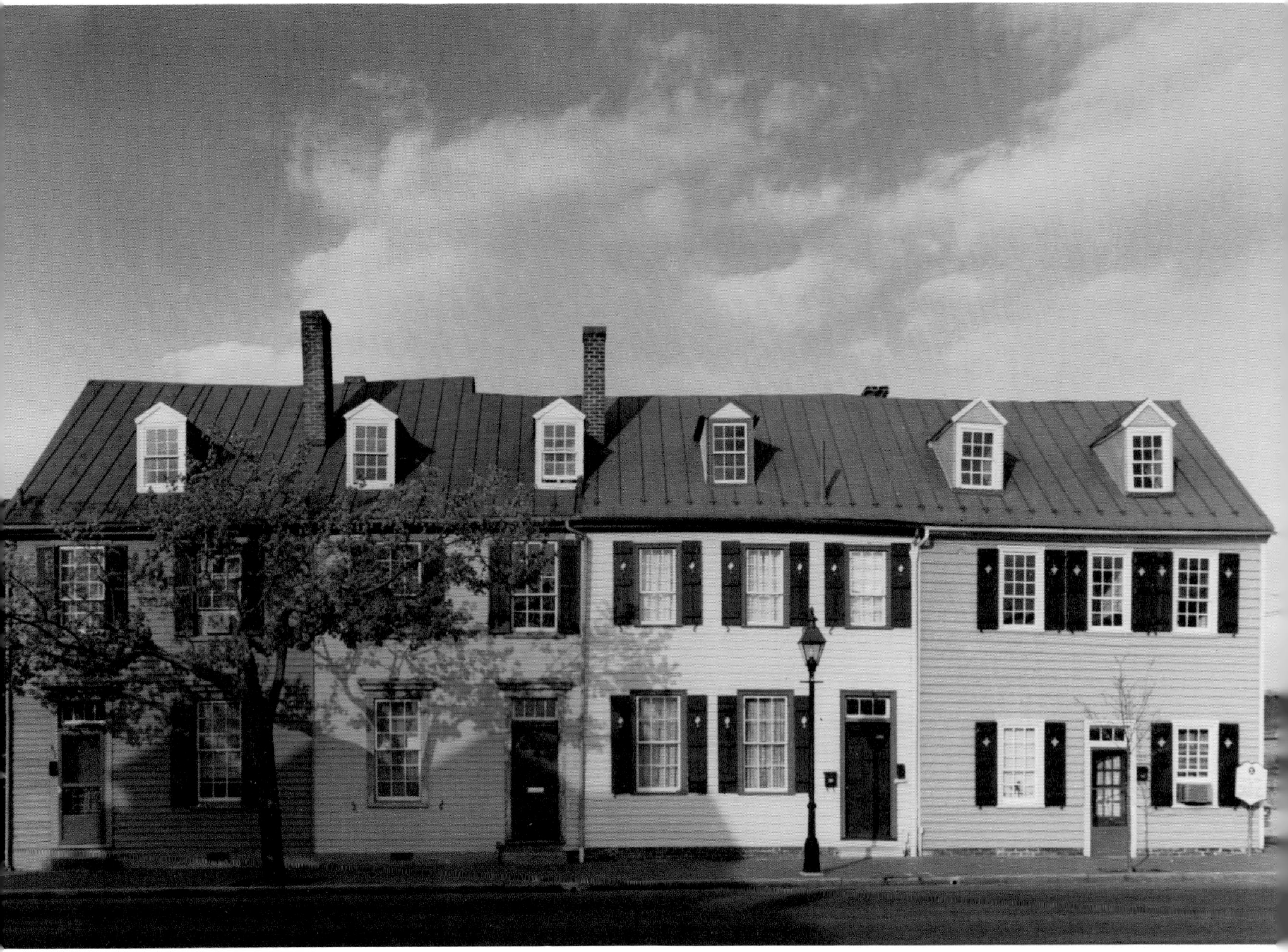

34

43 **Caroline Street Residences**

These early nineteenth century row houses, near the railroad station on Caroline Street, are typical of the small scale buildings in the center of the town. The house at right was once a grocery store. The early twentieth century view by Frances Benjamin Johnston shows how little change has taken place in the intervening years.

45 **Jones Row**

These three row houses, erected between 1839 and 1848 by a local grocer, Roy Jones, have been converted from derelict buildings into shops and apartments, now typical of the downtown area.

46 Nineteenth Century Row Houses

Along the area near the Fredericksburg Visitor Center in the 700 block of Caroline Street are many excellent brick houses—almost unaltered above the ground floor—from the first half of the nineteenth century. It is these houses which form the basis for the contemporary movement toward renovation and restoration of Fredericksburg's architectural heritage.

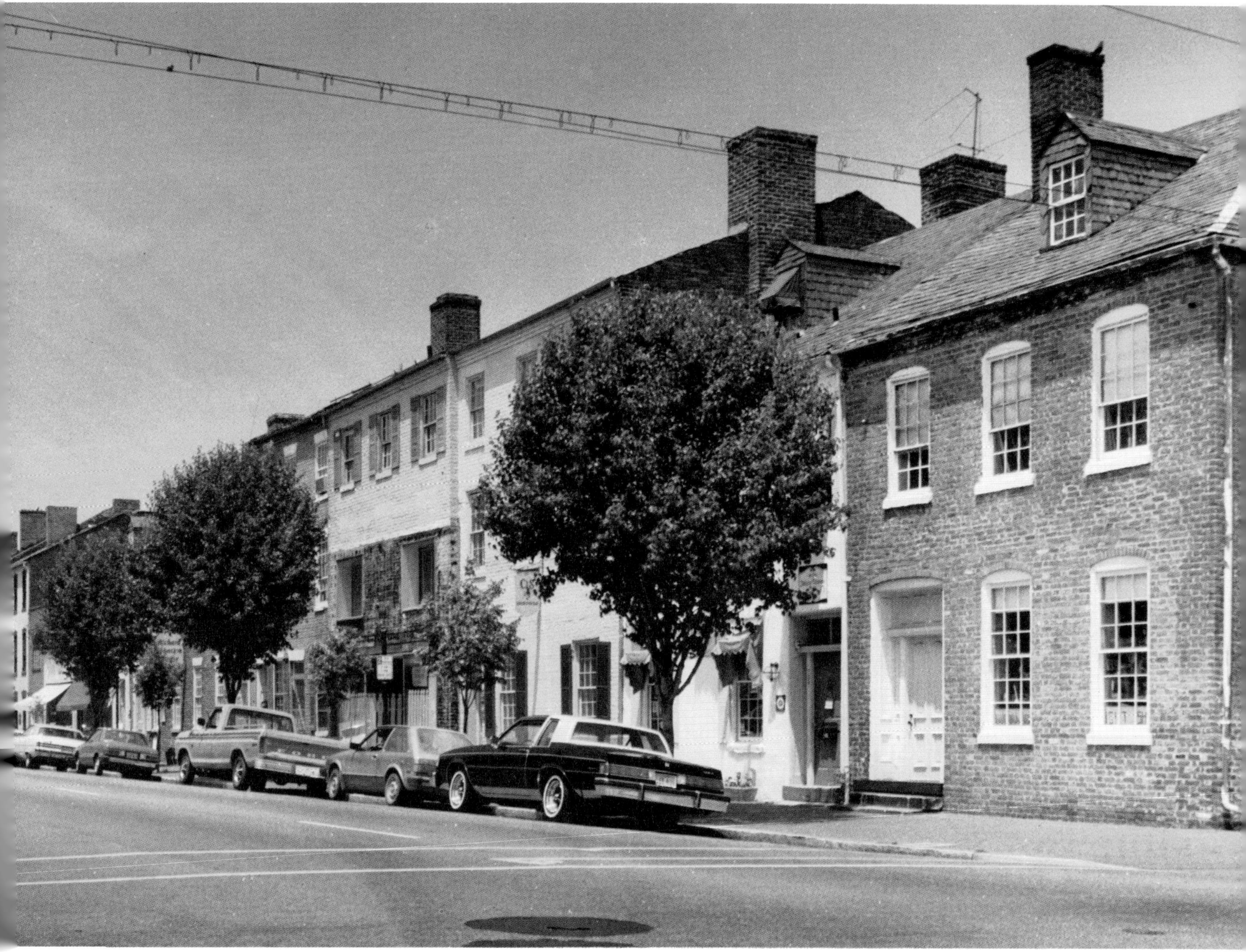

47 Dr. Hugh Mercer's Apothecary Shop

The eighteenth century shop of Hugh Mercer, a friend of George Washington and a general in his army, is one of four Fredericksburg houses owned by the Association for the Preservation of Virginia Antiquities. The shop displays medicines, apothecary jars and medical accessories from the Revolutionary era. New brick walks, trees and the removal of overhead wires in front of the house have given the shop a more dignified setting.

49 James Monroe's Law Office

James Monroe, the nation's fifth president, began his first law practice in Fredericksburg in 1786 in a modest brick building on Charles Street. During his three years in the town, he resided at 301 Caroline Street, a house owned by his uncle, Judge Joseph Jones. At the museum-law office are furniture and other memorabilia related to Monroe. At the rear is a presidential library erected here in 1962. A bust of Monroe by Margaret French Cresson watches over the site from the memorial garden in the yard.

50 M.S. Chancellor Outbuilding

Library of Congress

51 M. S. Chancellor's Store. In the early twentieth century the firm of M. S. Chancellor operated "The Farmers Store" at the corner of William and Charles Streets. Hardware and agricultural supplies were displayed daily on the public sidewalk.

Quaint old brick outbuildings stretched down Charles Street behind the store, looking here much as they must have in the early nineteenth century when they were built. The Chancellor Store complex was demolished in the 1950s.

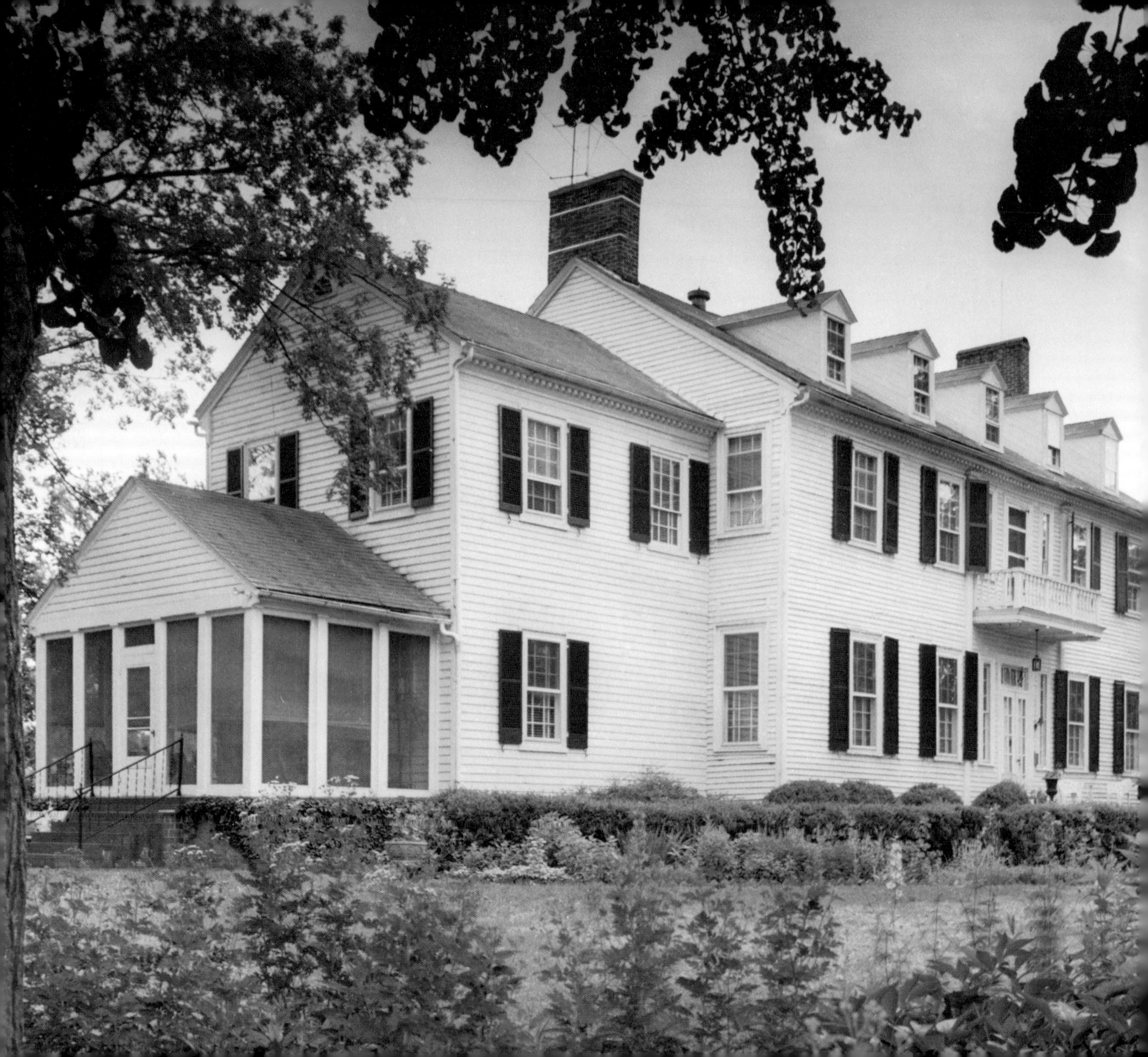

52 Federal Hill

One of the most beloved houses in the town occupies a hillside site once outside the town limit. Federal Hill has an illustrious history. Its interior design was inspired by William Buckland's work at Gunston Hall. Frances Benjamin Johnston captured the interior detail in 1927. The Johnston collection at the Library of Congress includes many other photographs of the interior and the exterior of Federal Hill. The lawn and gardens are among the finest in town and each spring bring forth a new bounty of blossom and fragrance to Hanover Street, now no longer rural.

Library of Congress

54

54 Hanover Street

A Greek Revival house with massive fluted columns and its neighbor, a Federal style brick house, both from the second quarter of the nineteenth century.

55 Carmichael House, 1780

Named after the Carmichael family, owners for over a century. The elegant Georgian porch with stone step and iron bootscraper adorns the main entrance to several apartments.

56

National Park Service

56 Gazebo

An old gazebo on Hanover Street, which was disassembled and moved to Stafford County.

57 Hanover Street, with Brompton in Background

This brick house on Hanover Street was here during the heavy fighting during the occupation of Fredericksburg. Now gone, the house was photographed by a neighbor early in the twentieth century.

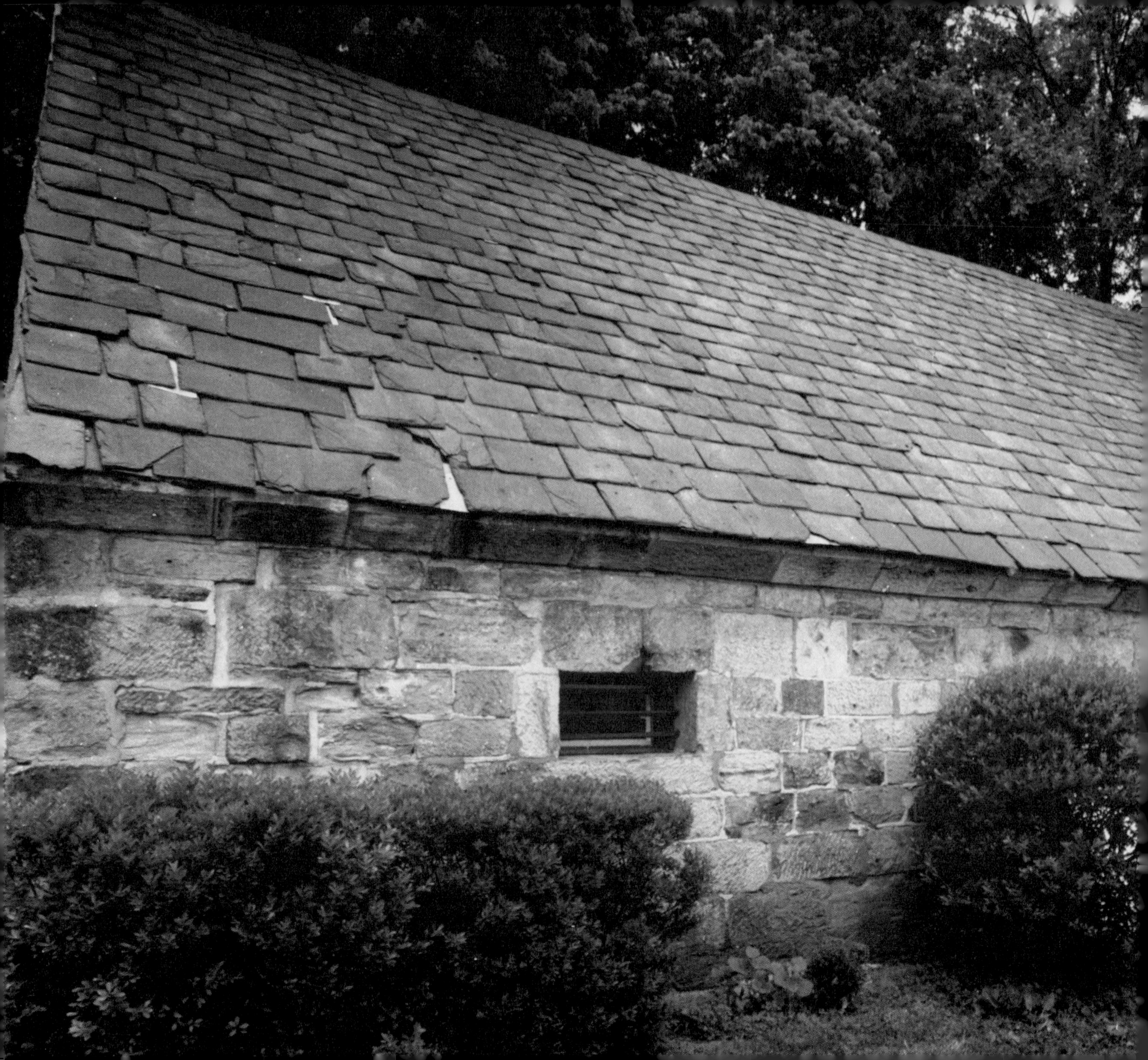

58 Old Stone Warehouse

The oldest masonry building in the city, the Old Stone Warehouse, on the Rappahannock, is the only surviving warehouse originally built to serve the port of Fredericksburg.

59 **New City Hall**

After 168 years in old City Hall the city government moved into the former United States Post Office in 1982. An example of the town's preference for adaptive reuse of its older buildings, the new City Hall contains office space for all the city's administrative offices and the City Council. Designed by James Knox Taylor and built in 1909, the Post Office was enlarged in 1937.

60 **Dormer Windows, Chimneys on Caroline Street**

The dormers, windows and old brick chimneys of old Fredericksburg remain in the business section of Caroline Street. Many of these buildings now feature apartments upstairs in what had been vacant spaces. Most of the brick buildings seen here date from the period after the fire of 1807.

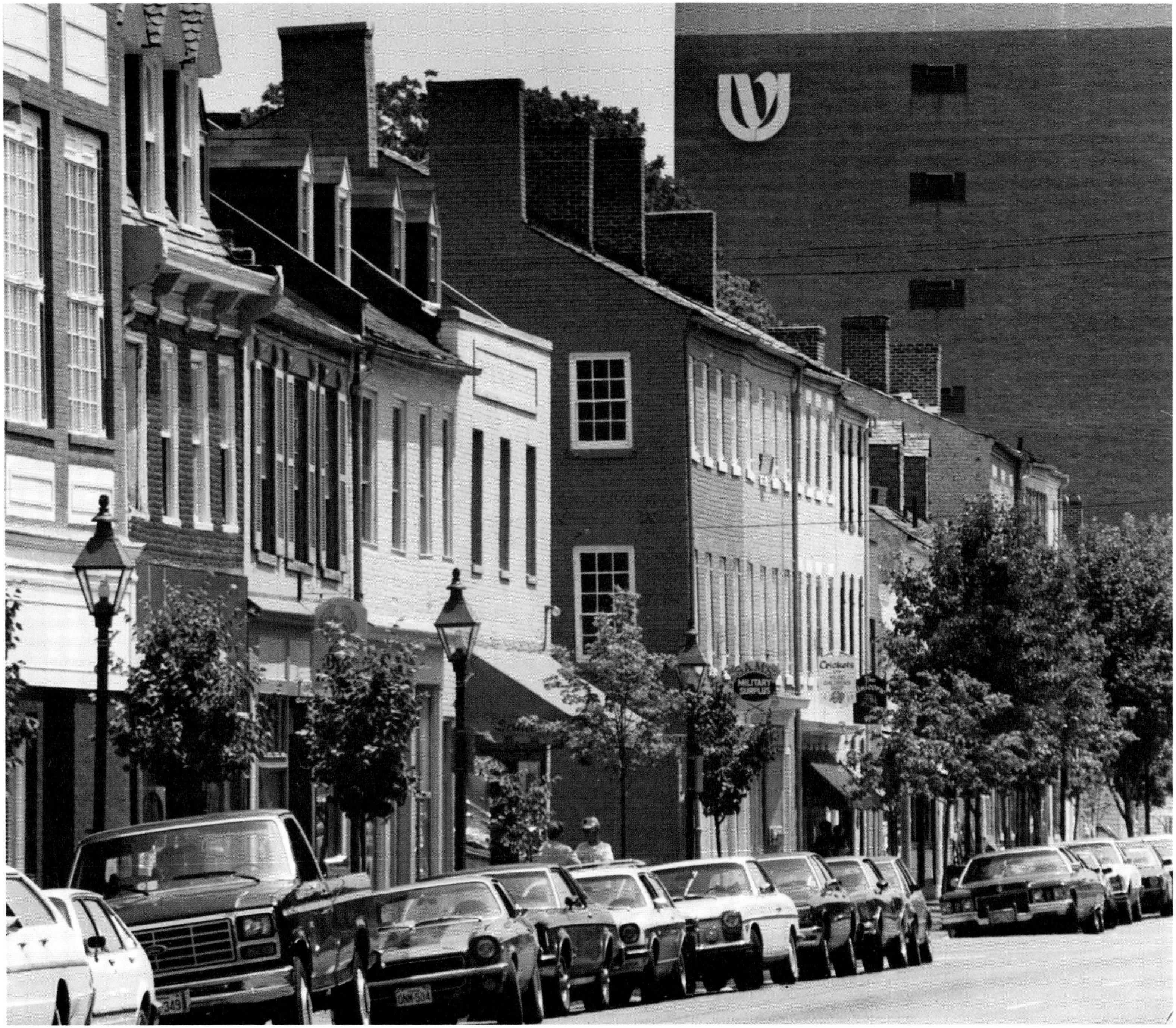
MILITARY SURPLUS
Crickets

Exchange Hotel   Enterprise Building

Main Street, looking North, Fredericksburg, Va.

Historic Fredericksburg Foundation Inc.

62 Contemporary view of Caroline Street

63 Twenty years ago both these early twentieth century houses on Caroline Street were in decline. The corner building now houses a retail store and an apartment with contemporary skylights. The other house is a single family dwelling recently restored.

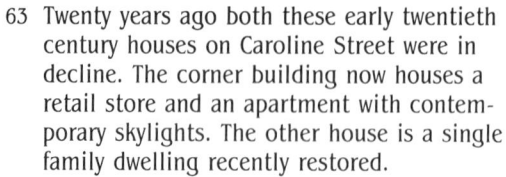

64 **Once a Duplex**

Constructed as a duplex house in the 1880s and then used by a locally-famous bootlegger, this Amelia Street dwelling has been restored and enlarged for one family.

65 **Geo. W. B. Spooner House and Rising Sun Tavern**

George W. B. Spooner married into the family of the tavern owner, Gustavus B. Wallace. Between 1792 and 1794, after the marriage, Spooner built his residence on Wallace's former lot next to the Tavern. The interior of the house has fine Federal detailing, with reeded cornice, a mantel and overmantel, and raised panel doors. Vacant for over six years and in severely deteriorated condition, the Spooner House is being restored as a private residence. In the original house plan, the first floor room on Caroline Street was used as a general store. The ceiling beams are still clad with beaded pine boards. The Rising Sun Tavern was in use until the middle of the nineteenth century.

65

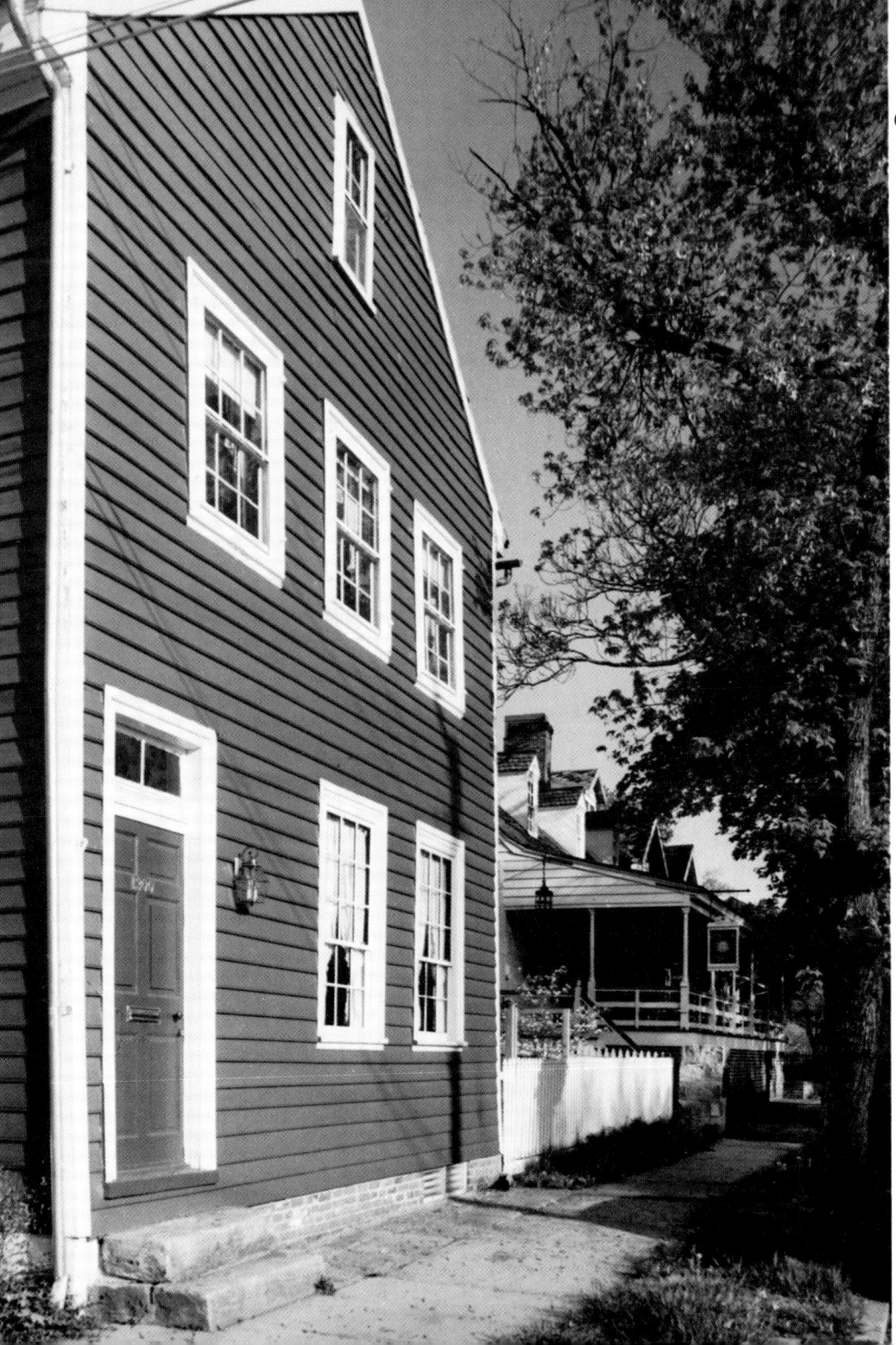

67 68

56

67 **Rising Sun Tavern**

Originally the residence of Charles Washington, youngest brother of George Washington, the building became a tavern about 1790. This room probably would have been Washington's Drawing Room. The house has corner fireplaces in several rooms.

68 An old globe, a horse-measuring scale, a safe and a mousetrap in the Tavern-keepers office.

69 A table set up for games in the Tap Room

71 An Old Brick Kitchen, Fauquier Street

Now a residence, this old kitchen building from the late eighteenth century or early nineteenth century probably was part of a house complex no longer standing.

72 New Uses for Old Houses

These two frame houses of the nineteenth century have found new life as an antique shop with residence above and an office. Nearly lost to demolition, they were saved following a public outcry.

73 The Second Oldest House

Begun in the 1740s by John Allan, a merchant, the second oldest house in Fredericksburg has been owned by the same family since 1882. A major addition—the north end of the house—in 1829 and other changes made over the years make the house more suitable for contemporary living. Among the many features of the house are seven fireplaces, a large country kitchen and a screened porch at the rear.

74

75

74 **Second Oldest House**

Entrance hall and stair from the rear. A Federal soldier, shot dead at the bottom of this stair, is buried in the yard.

75 Living Room

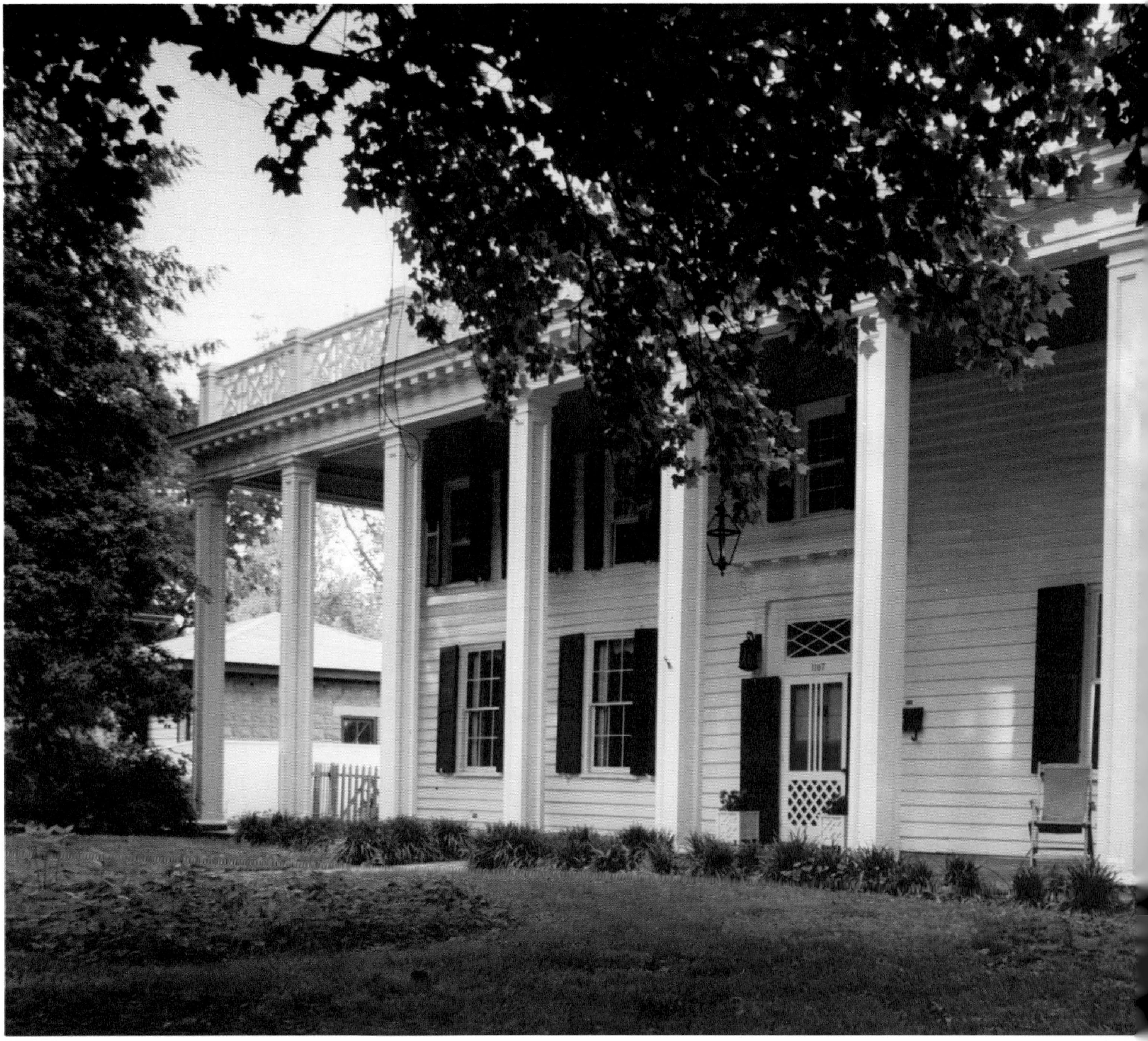

76 Charles Dick House

Part of this colonnaded house, set well back from busy Princess Anne Street, is said to be the oldest dwelling in the town and the residence of Charles Dick, a commissioner of the Revolutionary War gunnery near the town. The south end of the house is built of stone. The massive porch and balustrade was added in the early 1900s. Presidents Washington, Cleveland and Coolidge are known to have visited there.

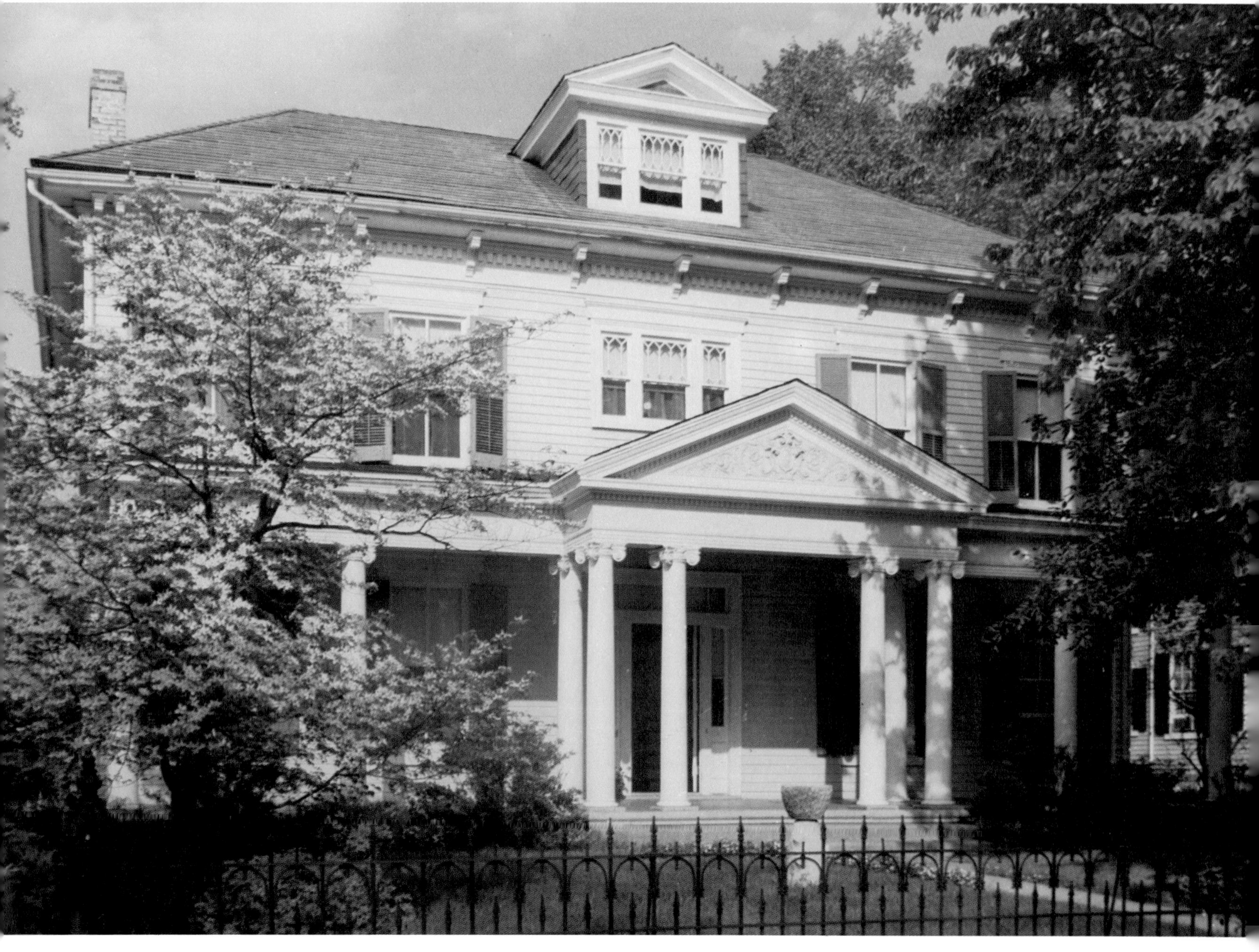

64

77 Georgian Revival

The Georgian style, so popular among Virginians in the eighteenth century, came around again in the early twentieth century. In this house on Princess Anne Street the triple sashes of the dormer and the relief carving on the portico are especially fine examples of the style.

78 Bed and Breakfast

An old private residence on Princess Anne Street has a new life as a small hotel, The Kenmore Inn. Built in 1824 by an unmarried woman, Miss Rebecca Tayloe Lomax, the house has been a rooming house for the elderly, a coffee shop, and a Mexican restaurant. The style of the house repeats the pattern established by two of its neighbors across Princess Anne Street. Doswell House is at left.

79 A Federal House Rescued

One of four brick Federal-style homes at the corner of Princess Anne and Lewis Streets, this house once had a coat of paint and a massive Victorian porch across the front and side, obscuring its true Federal heritage. A new garden wall and landscaping were added during the restoration. The house was built about 1818.

81 Doswell House, iron work on porch

80 Doswell House and Iron Tracery Porch

The Doswell House, named in honor of its Civil War owner, James T. Doswell, was once said to be an eighteenth century building. New research has established 1838 as the correct date. The ironwork tracery on the porch features a corn motif, shown in detail elsewhere in this book. In the background is the second oldest house in the town. Doswell House is on the southeast corner of Princess Anne and Lewis Street.

82 Mackey's Folly

It is said that building this house in 1817 sent owner Robert Mackey into bankruptcy, thus the name "Mackey's Folly." Also called Shepperd House in honor of the family which owned the building for almost a century after the Civil War, it is one of four important Federal buildings on a prominent downtown corner. The additions on the east side were built in the Victorian manner.

83 Hugh Martin's House

Confederate veteran Dr. Hugh Martin built this exceptionally handsome and sturdy frame house on Princess Anne Street about 1890. The house has survived changes of use without major alteration of the exterior. The porch, the Italianate brackets and cornice are original.

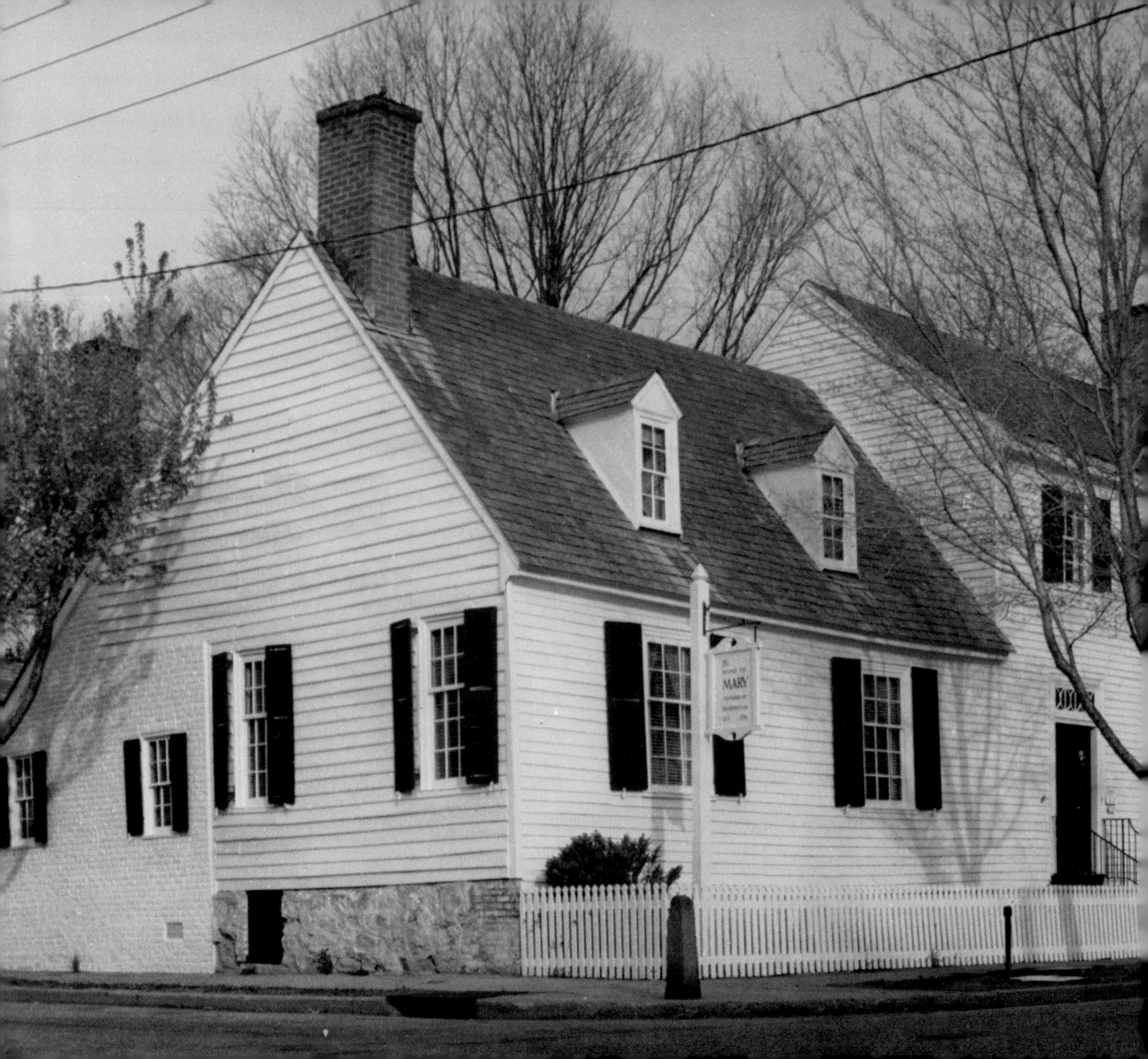
MARY

84 Mrs. Washington's House on Charles Street

Among the most popular museum houses in the town is the frame house on Charles Street purchased by George Washington for his mother, Mary Washington, in 1772. The one-and-a-half story and two-story sections (at left) are part of the original house. Mrs. Washington died here in 1789. Her home is now owned by the Association for the Preservation of Virginia Antiquities. A lovely eighteenth century garden in the rear yard was a project of the Garden Club of Virginia.

Central Rappahannock Regional Library

85 Mary Washington House in 1927.

When Frances Benjamin Johnston photographed the town in 1927, the Mary Washington House still had its front porch and tin roof, all removed during later restoration.

86 Jane Howison Beale, born just around the corner at St. James House, spent most of her life in this house at the corner of Charles and Lewis Street, across from the Mary Washington House. Mrs. Beale's diary of her life after her husband's death was published by Historic Fredericksburg Foundation in 1979. The diary covers the years between 1850 and 1862 and includes a vivid account of the battle over the town of Fredericksburg in December 1862.

73

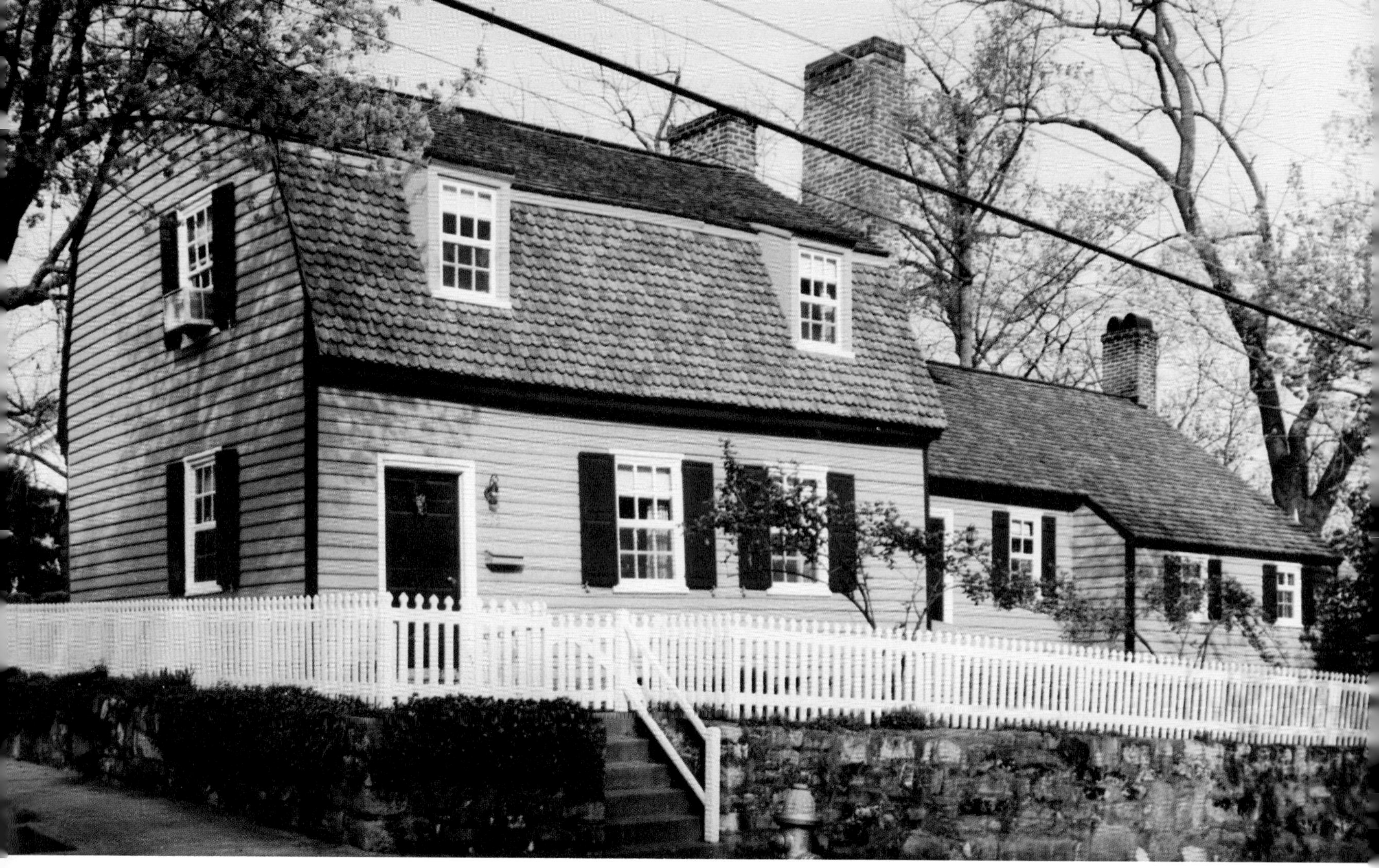

87 **St. James House**

St. James, a pre-Revolutionary building erected by James Mercer, an attorney, is an outstanding example of the small scale home popular in Fredericksburg in the eighteenth century. Small, yet comfortable, the St. James House is now a residence owned by the Association for the Preservation of Virginia Antiquities. Now restored and open to the public twice a year, during Garden Week and again in October, or by appointment for special tours, the house was decaying and neglected in the 1960s when it was purchased by W. H. Tolerton and Daniel Breslin, two antique dealers. They restored the house and donated it to the APVA. In the photographs of the house by Frances Benjamin Johnston are the Victorian trimwork removed during the restoration.

88 Garden at St. James House

90

90 **St. James House**

Dining Room with eighteen century antique furnishings

91 A portrait of Frederick, Prince of Wales, after whom the town was named, hangs over the Drawing Room mantel. The frame for the portrait includes the seal of the Prince.

92 Garden gate

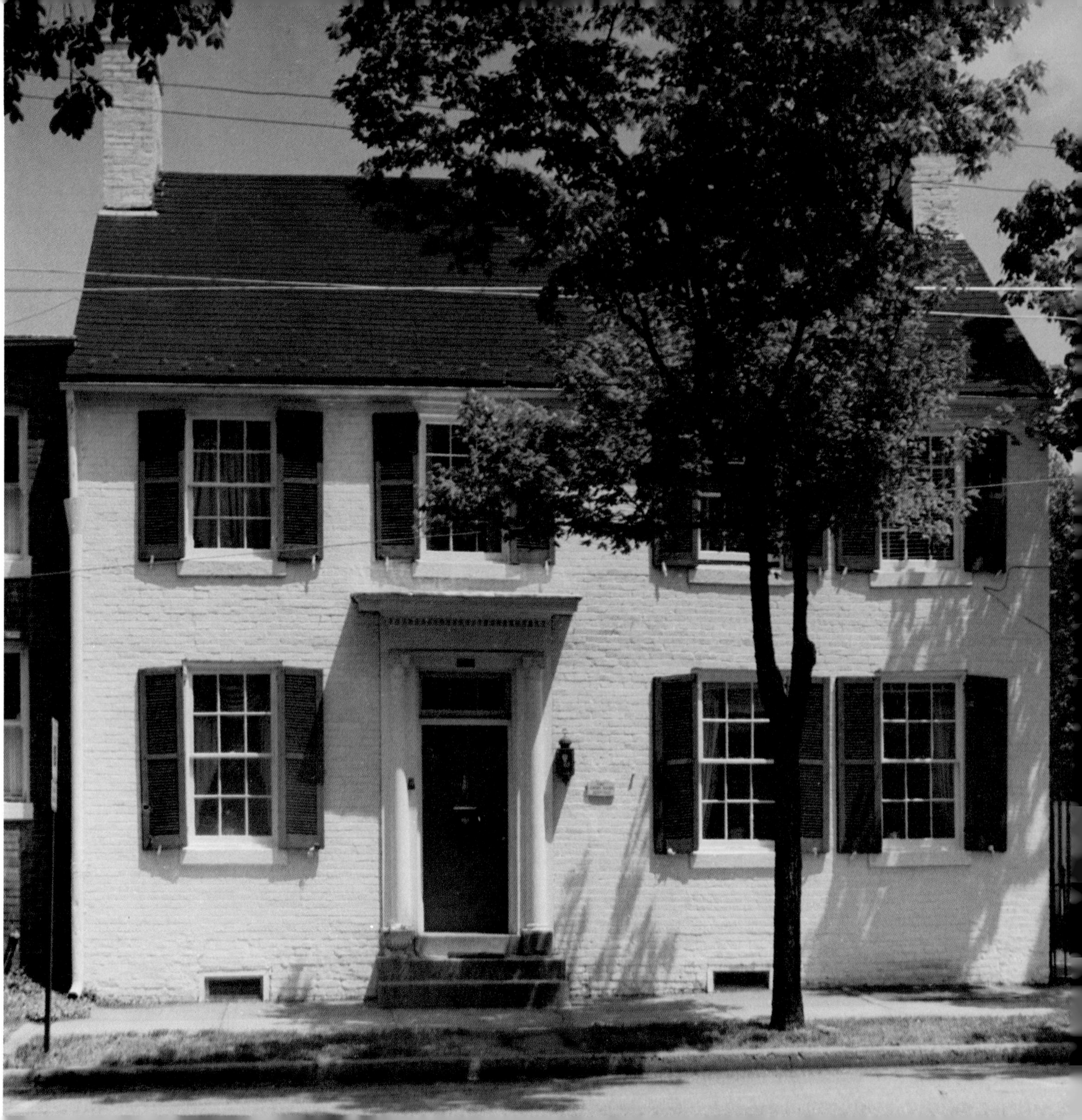

93 Traditional Architecture on Charles Street

The persistence of popular architectural styles is illustrated by this 1857 house on Charles Street. Federal themes are echoed in the shape of the house, its windows and in the columns flanking the entrance doorway. This may have been one of the last houses built in that style before the outbreak of the Civil War.

94 A Federal House on Amelia Street

Originally a private residence and now a professional office building, the Doggett House has graced the corner of Amelia and Princess Anne Street, opposite the Baptist Church, since about 1820. The house contains fine examples of Federal style architectural ornamentation in its interior rooms. Doggett House was named after Kate Doggett Boggs, whose family owned the house when Frances Benjamin Johnston photographed the property in 1927. Miss Doggett's antique shop, whose sign is seen at left the old photograph, was in "The Quarters," a handsome dependency on the southwest corner of the lot.

96 Smithsonia

The Presbyterians of Fredericksburg built this house in 1834 as an aslyum for female orphans. The style of *Smithsonia* reflects the popularity of Greek Revival architecture. The building is now a private residence, but it has also served as a boys' dormitory for the Fredericksburg College, a boys' school no longer in existence

97 A private garden with forged iron gate, Smithsonia

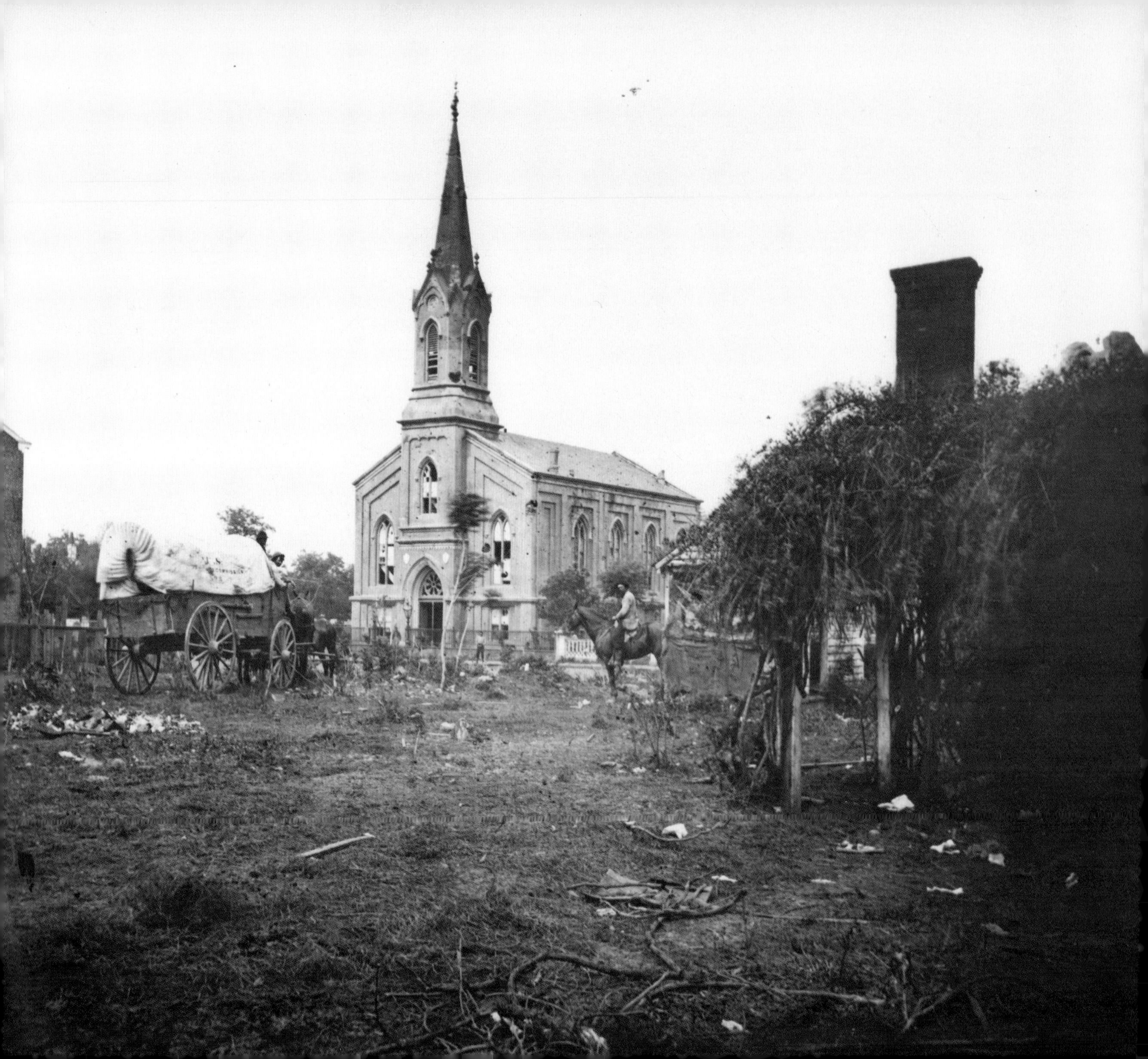

98 Fredericksburg Baptist Church

The newly-erected Fredericksburg Baptist Church was among the many casualties of the rain of shells and cannon balls which fell upon the city during the Battle of Fredericksburg in December 1862. This photograph, from the "Brady Collection" at the Library of Congress, probably was taken in 1864 during Federal occupation of the town.

99 Fredericksburg Baptist Church from Smithsonia

The serenity of this scene contrasts sharply with the devastation in the 1862 photograph from the "Brady Collection" at the Library of Congress. The church was erected in 1855 in the popular Gothic-inspired Victorian style, first seen in Fredericksburg in the Courthouse and St. George's Episcopal Church.

99 Washington Avenue

After the turn of the century Washington Avenue was the most prestigious place in town in which to build a new house. The two imposing dwellings are among the best. The stone house was built about 1906 by Eugene Bode, a prosperous local businessman.

100 Major Embrey's Gift, Weselin

Major W. S. Embrey built this house on Prince Edward Street for his daughter Mae Embrey Rowlett around the turn of the century. The interior of the house has been redecorated and emphasizes faux marbre floors and sponge-painted walls.

101 **Weselin**
Entrance foyer with *faux marbre* design on the wood floors

102 Upper stair hall with stenciled wallpaper borders

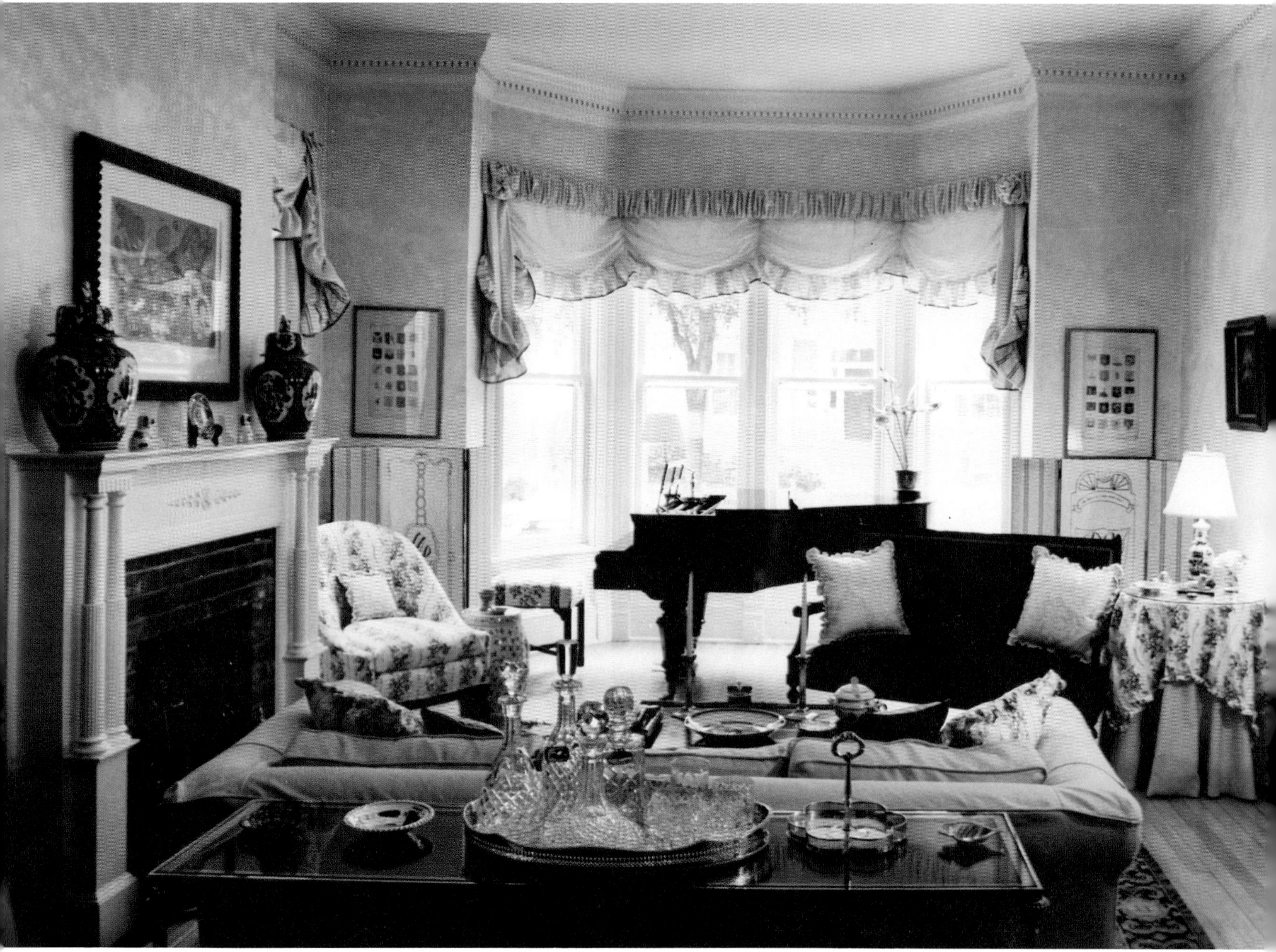

102 **Weselin**

A baby grand piano in the front bay window of the living room in this turn of the century house. The plaster walls are sponge-painted.

103 **A Melange of Styles**

On Prince Edward Street is the "Spinning House," an old stone house, now enlarged, associated with Mary Washington. To the left is a handsome Victorian residence with English basement.

104 Spinning House, 1927

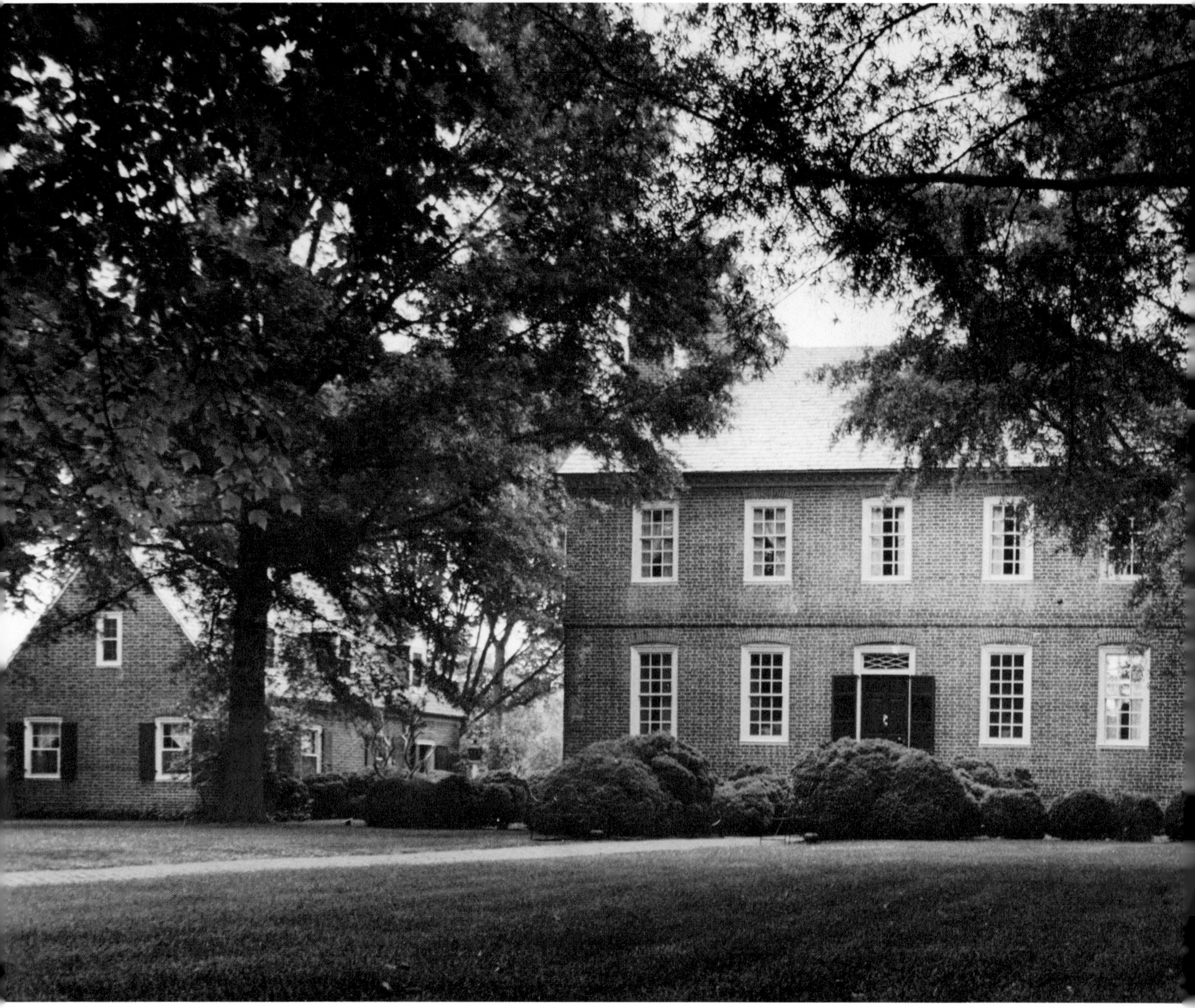

106 Kenmore
The restored home of Fielding Lewis and Betty Washington Lewis, sister of George Washington, built about 1752. Kenmore's elaborate plasterwork interiors are of exceptional quality and beauty. The house has been refurbished based upon new research.

107 Kenmore
Stair hall, looking into the Drawing Room

109 **Kenmore**

The ornamental plaster ceiling in the Drawing Room, completed by an unknown French craftsman.

108 The Aesop's Fable overmantel in the Drawing Room

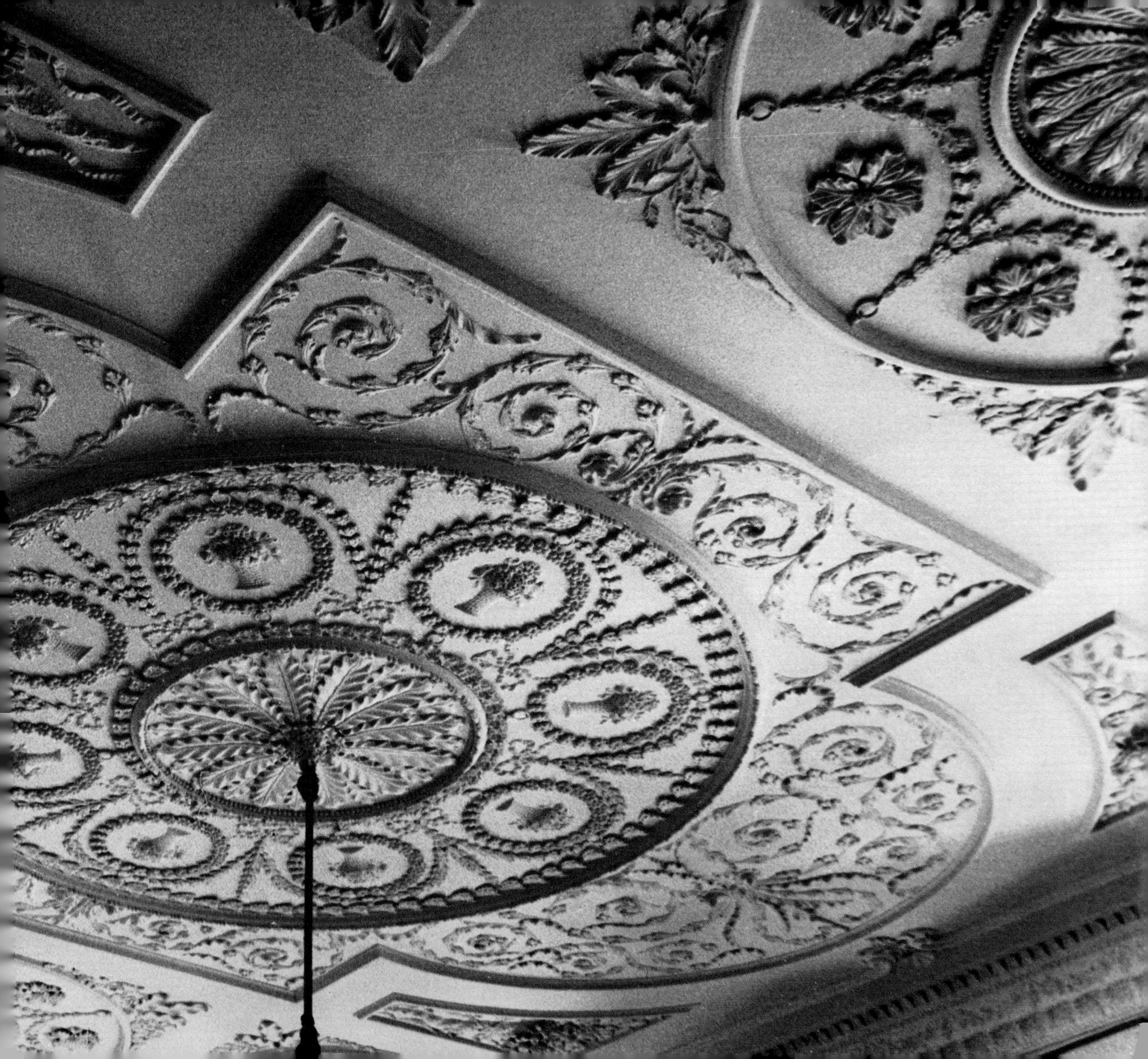

110 **Kenmore**

Eighteenth century secretary in the plantation office

111 **Hugh Mercer**

A monument on Washington Avenue in honor of General Hugh Mercer, a casualty of the Battle of Princeton, erected by the United States Congress in 1906.

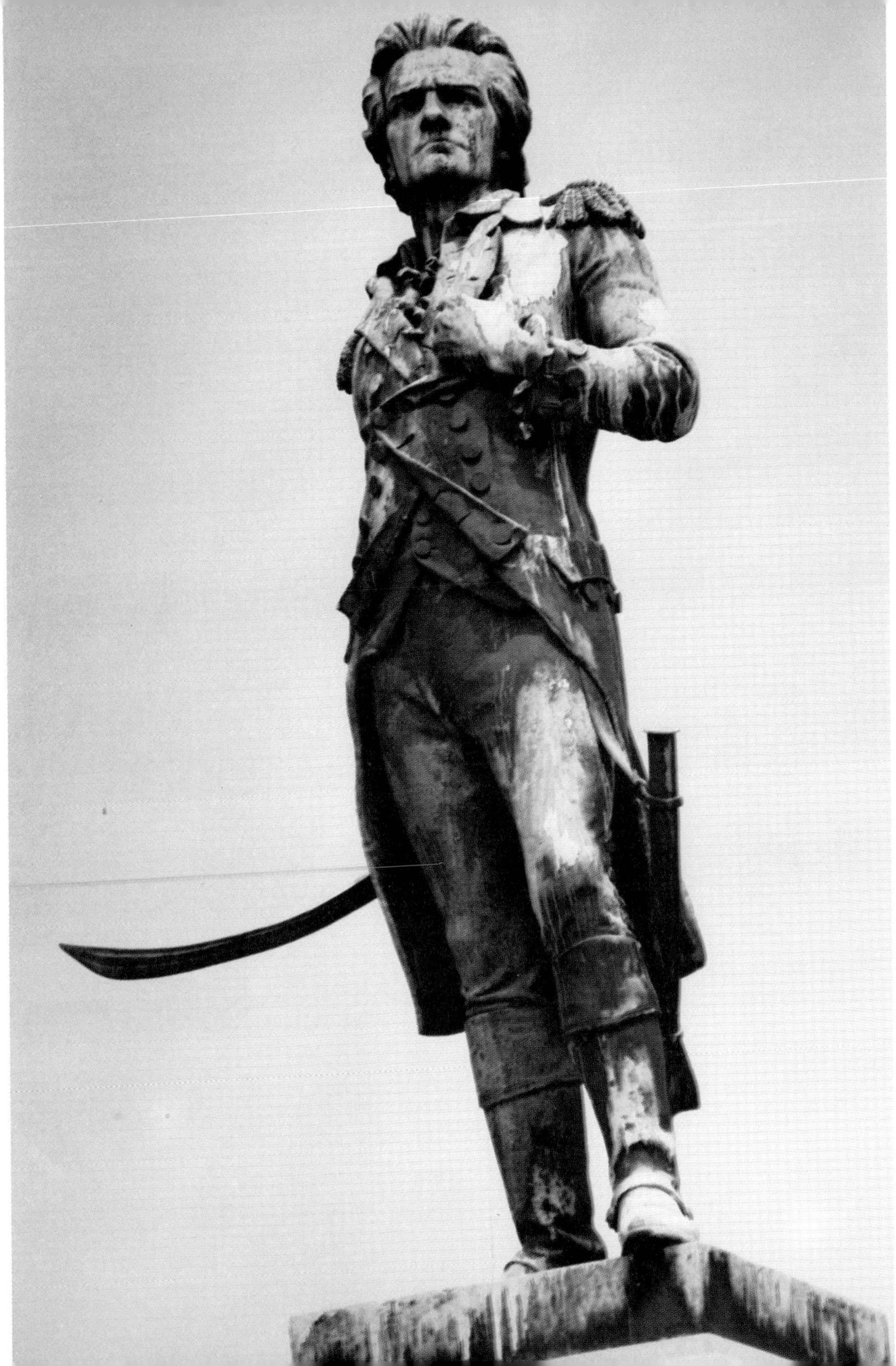
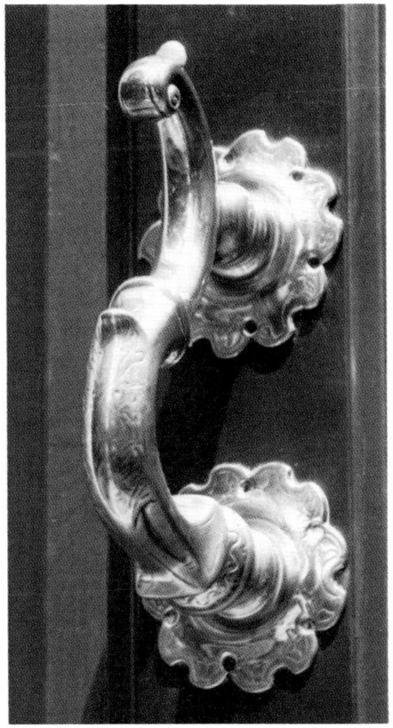
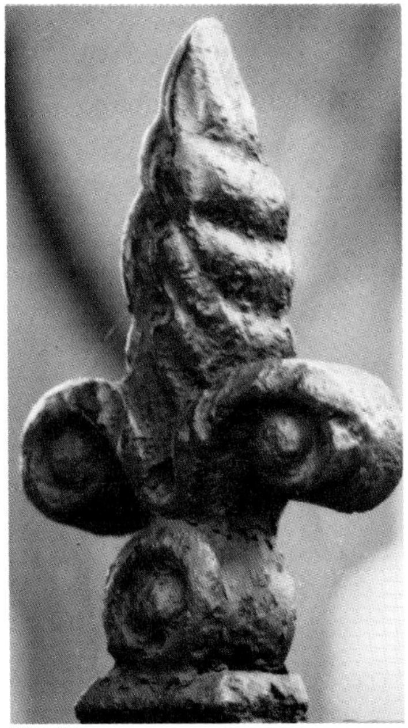

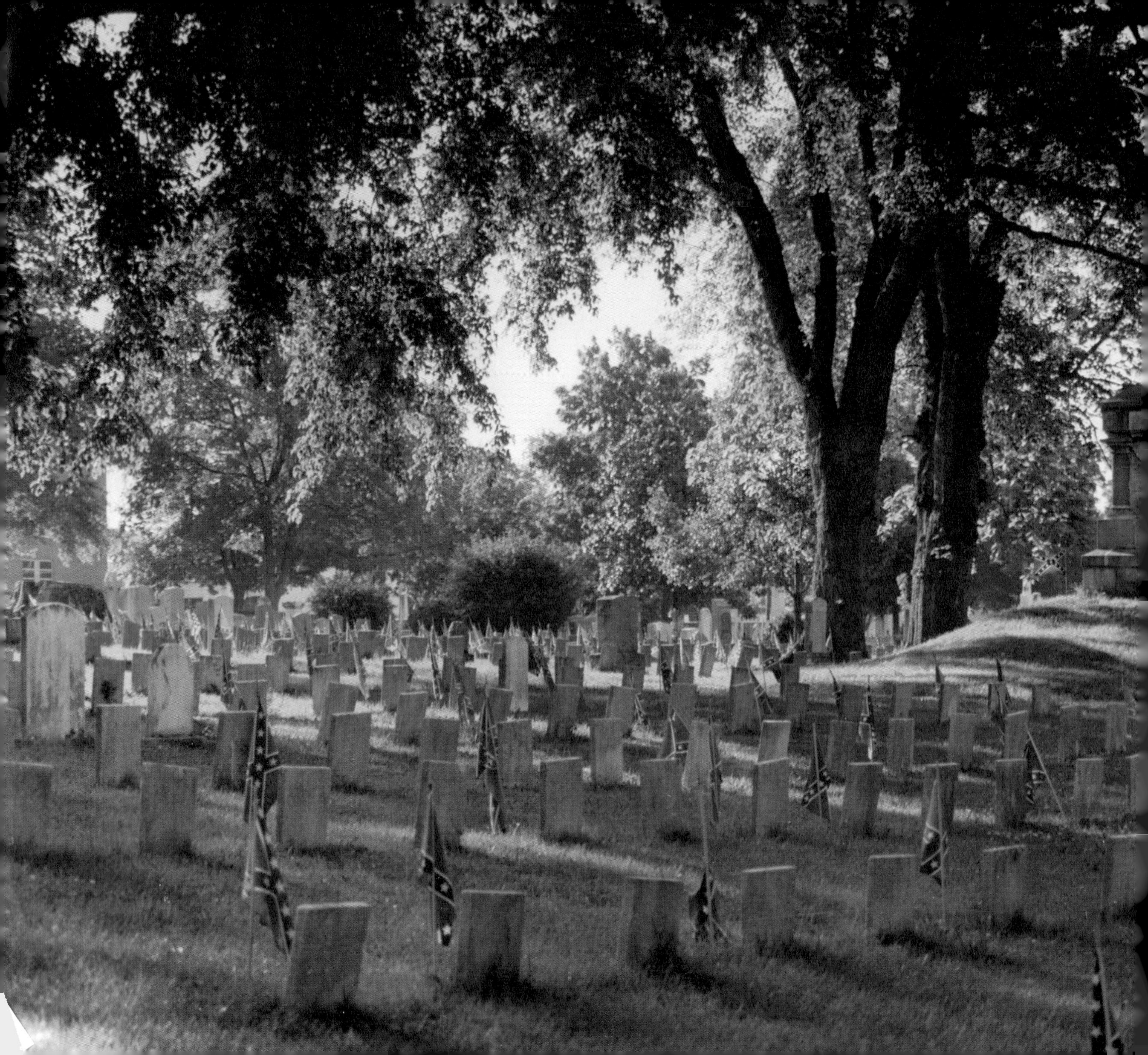

113 Confederate Cemetery on Memorial Day

Flags still flutter over the graves of veterans and their families on Memorial Day in the privately owned cemetery on Washington Avenue. The statue at right, installed in 1874, commemorates all Confederate dead.

114 Sgt. Richard Kirkland's heroic act on the battlefield of Fredericksburg in Felix De Welden's statue on Sunken Road.

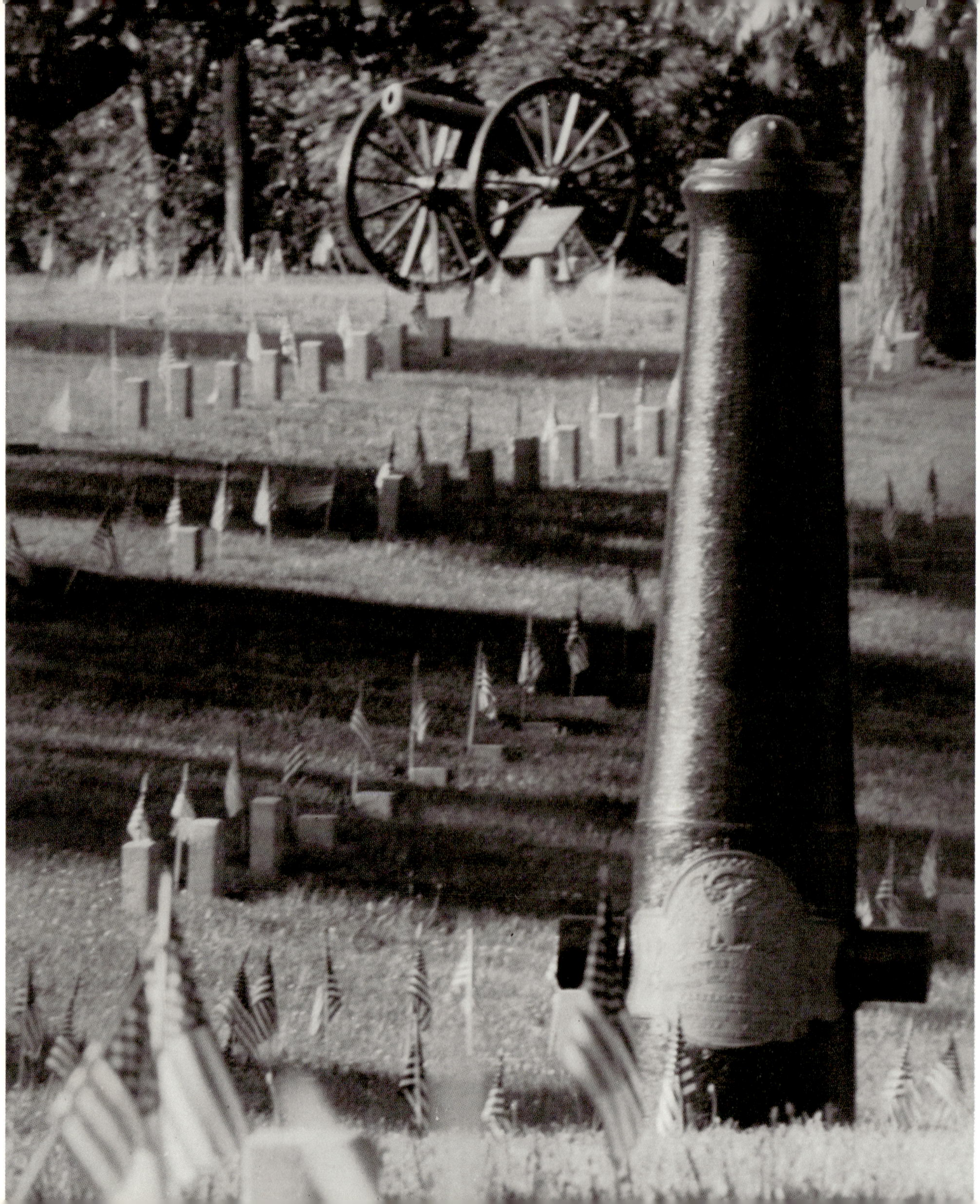

116 Rowe House, 1850s

The Reverend George Rowe, pastor at the newly constructed Fredericksburg Baptist Church, built his new house in the mid-1850s on Hanover Street in an area brought into the town in the 1851–1852 annexation. The area was part of the battlefield during the Federal assault on Sunken Road and Marye's Heights. Battle damage is still evident in the walls.

15 National Cemetery, where over 15,000 Federal casualties of the battles around Fredericksburg are buried. Many graves are marked only with numbered headstones.

117 118

Library of Congress

117 **The Proctor House, New Site**

Even in the eighteenth and nineteenth century Virginians were known for moving houses from one site to another. During the 1920s and 1930s several houses in the city of Fredericksburg were moved to avoid demolition. The Proctor House is seen here at its present site on Kenmore Avenue and at its original location on Princess Anne Street at Fauquier Street.

119 **Neri-Hallberg House**

The growth of a house and family is seen here in this frame house on Hanover Street. Once a field on the edge of town, this area is now filled with houses of the first half of our century.

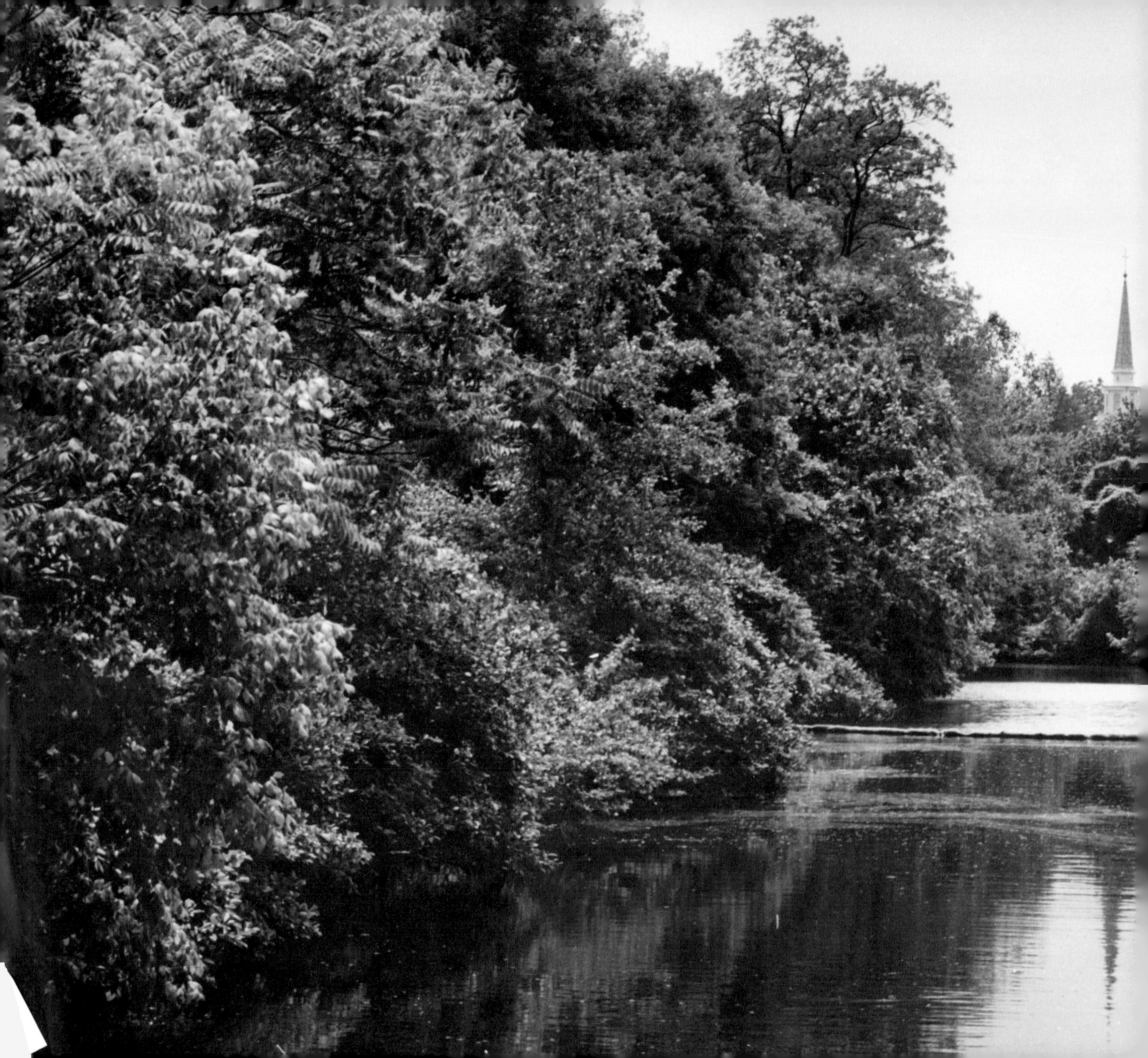

120 **The Canal, Reflecting the Christian Church Steeple**

The canal, part of the Rappahannock Navigation, was started in 1829. An extensive system of canals and locks, the Navigation bypassed the rapids at Fredericksburg. A three-mile section below the dam was rebuilt in the twentieth century to provide water for a power plant on upper Caroline Street. A bicycle path is planned for the old tow path.

Contemporary weathervane, Lewis Street

121 Cornell Street

A fine Federal house built in the 1930s on a site which had been open land a half-century earlier. Cornell Street is now in the center of the city.

122 Cornell Street Houses

Less than a century ago the site of these homes on Cornell Street near the College was a swampy area just west of the main part of the town. Drained and filled in the early twentieth century, the Kenmore Avenue valley includes an impressive display of Georgian Revival and Federal style homes.

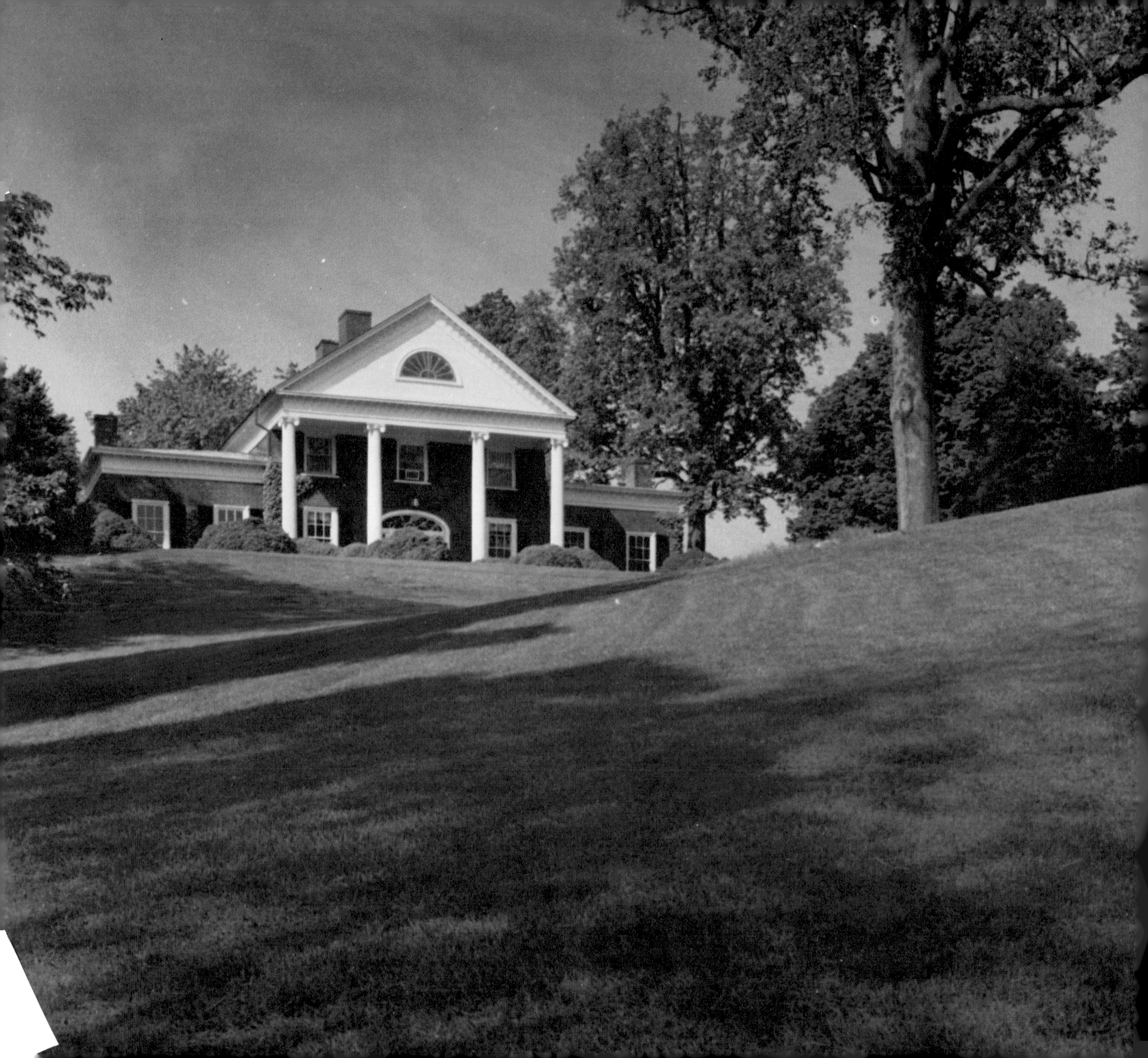

123 Brompton

The President of Mary Washington College now resides in the house once owned by Lt. Governor John L. Marye, Jr. The hill has been called "Marye's Heights" since the Civil War, when it was the site of Confederate gun emplacements. The original house, severely damaged during the war, was built in the late eighteenth century.

124

124 **Monroe Hall, at the College**

Mary Washington College occupies several of the prominent hills west of the old section of the town. One of the college's oldest structures is Monroe Hall, renovated by the college and its exterior appearance restored. Monroe Hall is the college's conference center.

125 **Howison House in the Battlefield Park**

The family of John and Robert Howison built this fine brick house in the countryside just beyond the town, probably hoping for a peaceful life, in the late 1850s. During the Battle of Fredericksburg their home was evacuated, owing to its location at the base of the hills where General Lee had his command post. Confederate trenches ran through the property. The house is still owned by a member of the Howison family.

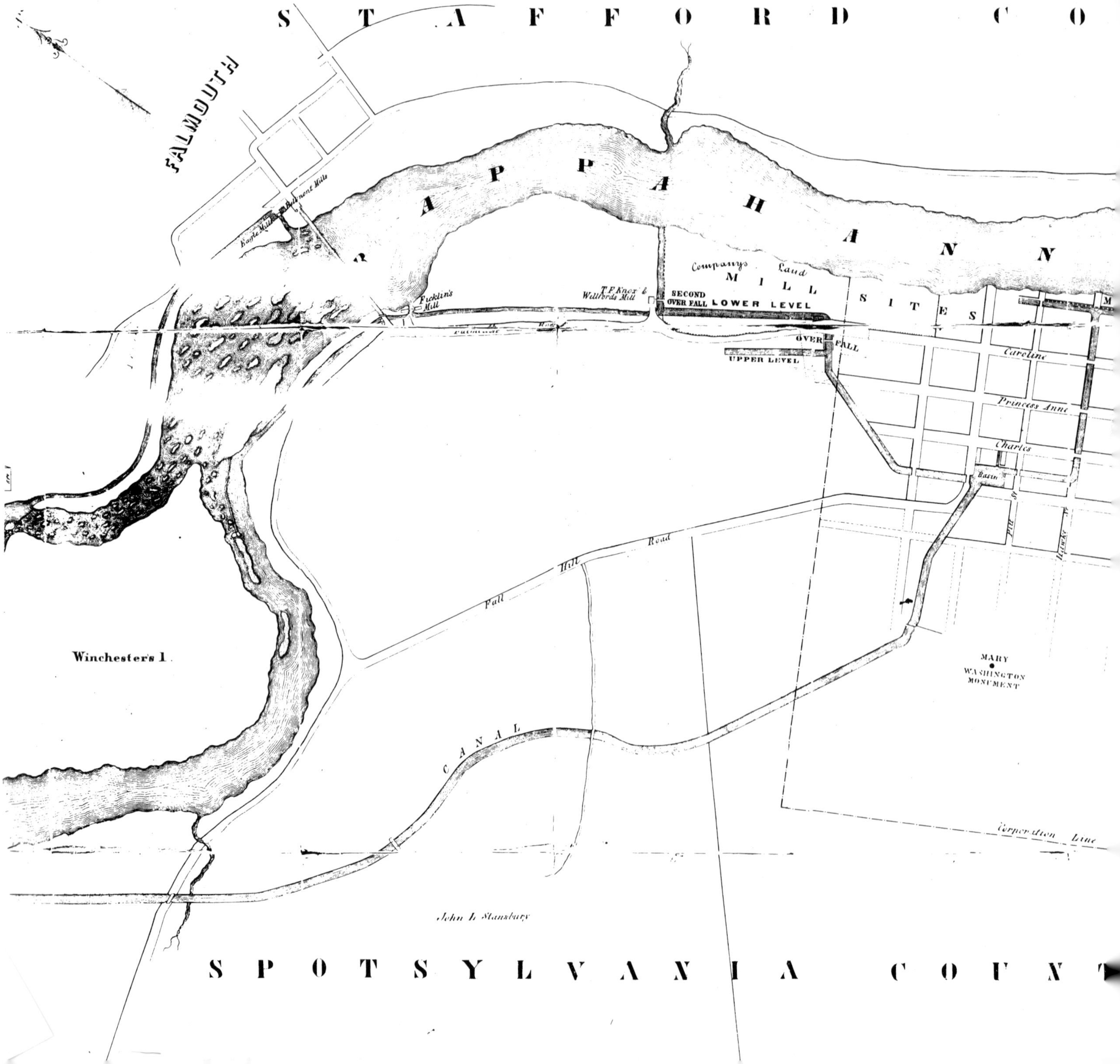

S T A F F O R D C O
FALMOUTH
Eagle Mill
Belmont Mills
R A P P A H A N N
Ficklin's Mill
T.F. Knox & Willfords Mill
SECOND OVER FALL
LOWER LEVEL
Companys Land
M I L L S I T E S
OVER FALL
UPPER LEVEL
Caroline
Princess Anne
Charles
Basin
Pitt St
Hawke St
Fall Hill Road
Winchester's I.
C A N A L
MARY WASHINGTON MONUMENT
Corporation Line
John L Stansbury
S P O T S Y L V A N I A C O U N T

OF THE CITY OF FREDERICKSBURG

With the Location of the

FRED'S'B'G WATER POWER CO'S
DAM, CANALS
and
MILL SITES

PLAN

of the South Abutment of the

FREDERICKSBURG WATER POWER CO'S
DAM

Scale 8 ft. to the inch

Elevation of A.A.

Vertical Section of Dam

Length of Dam 512 Ft.   Height of Dam 10 Ft.

MERCER SQR.

WILLIS HILL

Fredericksburg & Gordonsville R.R.

Brown's I.

Cemetery

128 Plant of the Bridgewater Milling Corporation.

129 The old Stone Warehouse remains today in downtown Fredericksburg, while its upriver contemporary, the Bridgewater Mill near Falmouth, was lost to demolition

130 **Basil Gordon House Artifact**

Bearing the initials "GR", probably George II, this large pottery fragment was found during an archeaological excavation at the Basil Gordon property in Falmouth in 1984. Part of a salt-glazed jug made in the Westerwald district of Germany in the late 18th century, this artifact is the largest yet found in the old Falmouth town. Basil Gordon was among the town's most prosperous merchants and landowners.

131 Old Falmouth

A brick house in Falmouth town on old road from Warrenton. Falmouth, Fredericksburg's sister town—both created in 1728—declined as Fredericksburg grew later in the eighteenth century.

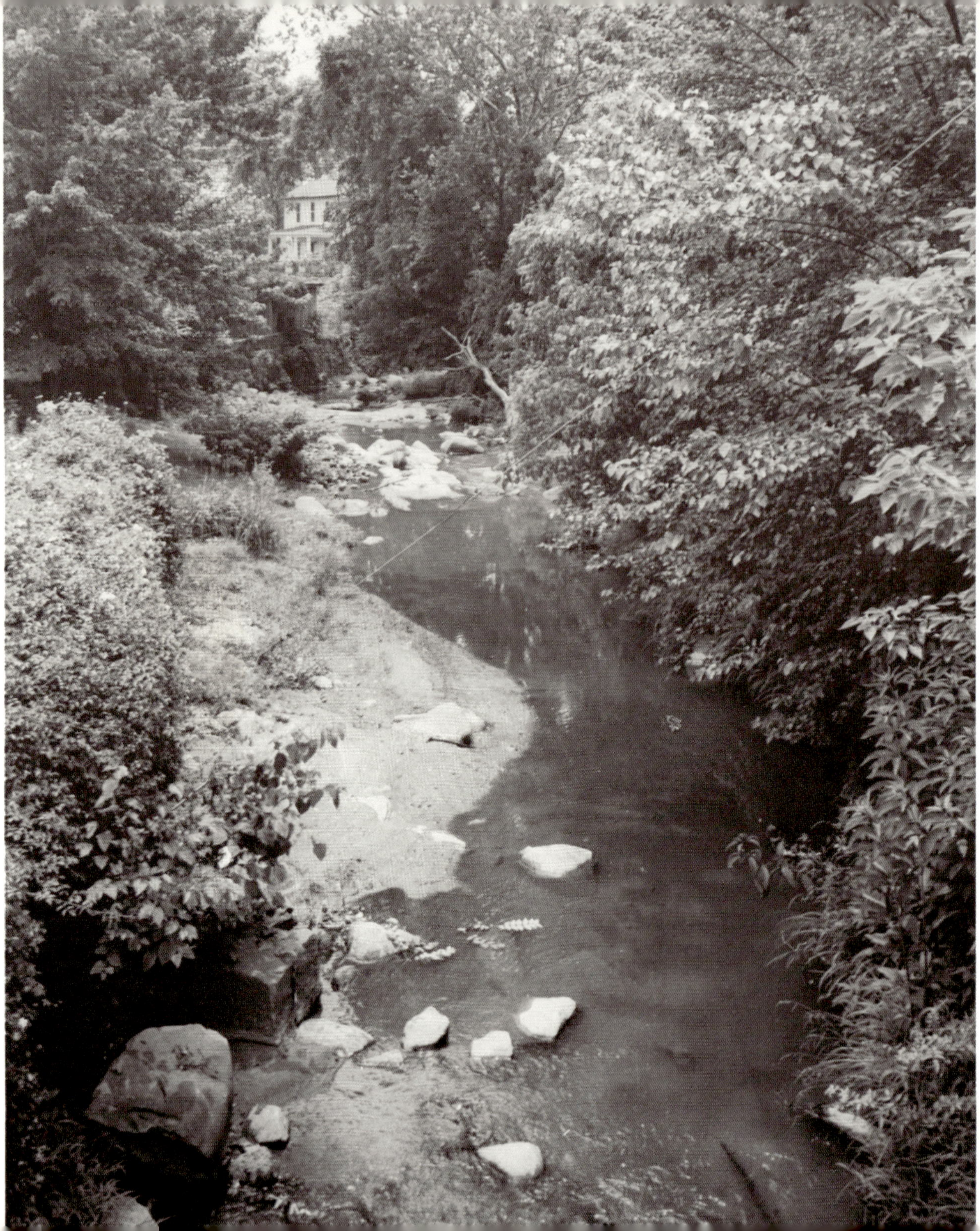

133 An old tavern in Falmouth, photographed in 1927 by Frances Benjamin Johnston.

National Park Service

134 Clearview, above Falmouth

Situated on one of the three prominent hills above Falmouth, Clearview can be seen for several miles from the Fredericksburg side of the river. The center part of the house was erected about 1790. The old photograph shows members of the Scott family and some of the estate's former slaves about 1890.

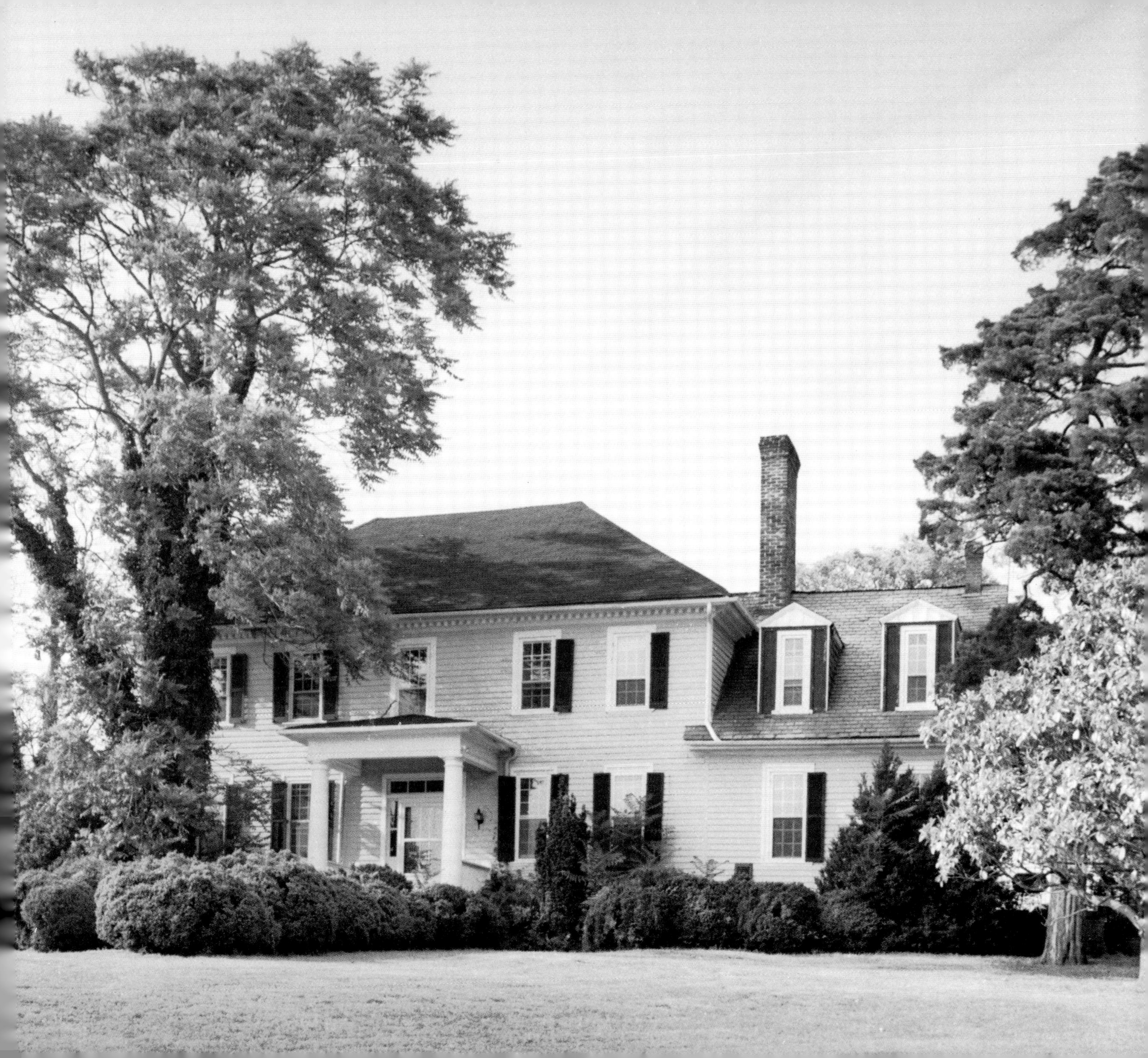

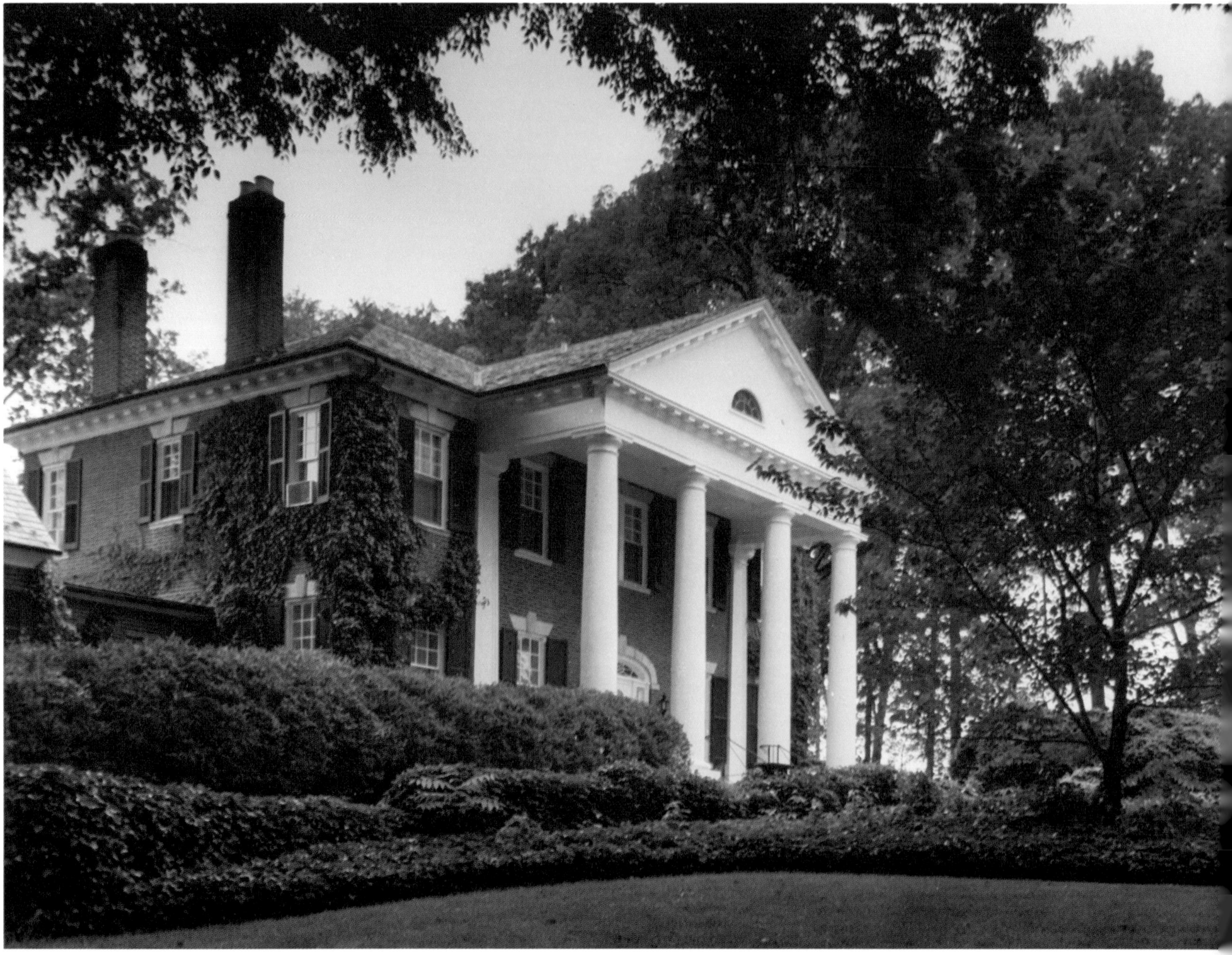

136 Snowden

At the top of one of the many sloping hills at the western end of the city is Snowden. The house, on one of the largest remaining undeveloped parcels of land in Fredericksburg, was built by George Benoit after 1926 when a fire destroyed the original house. The Snowden of today is a re-creation of the original building which had been built in 1808.

138 Snowden Pond

A fresh water pond below Snowden Farm is adjacent to two shopping centers and an apartment complex.

137 Snowden Cottage

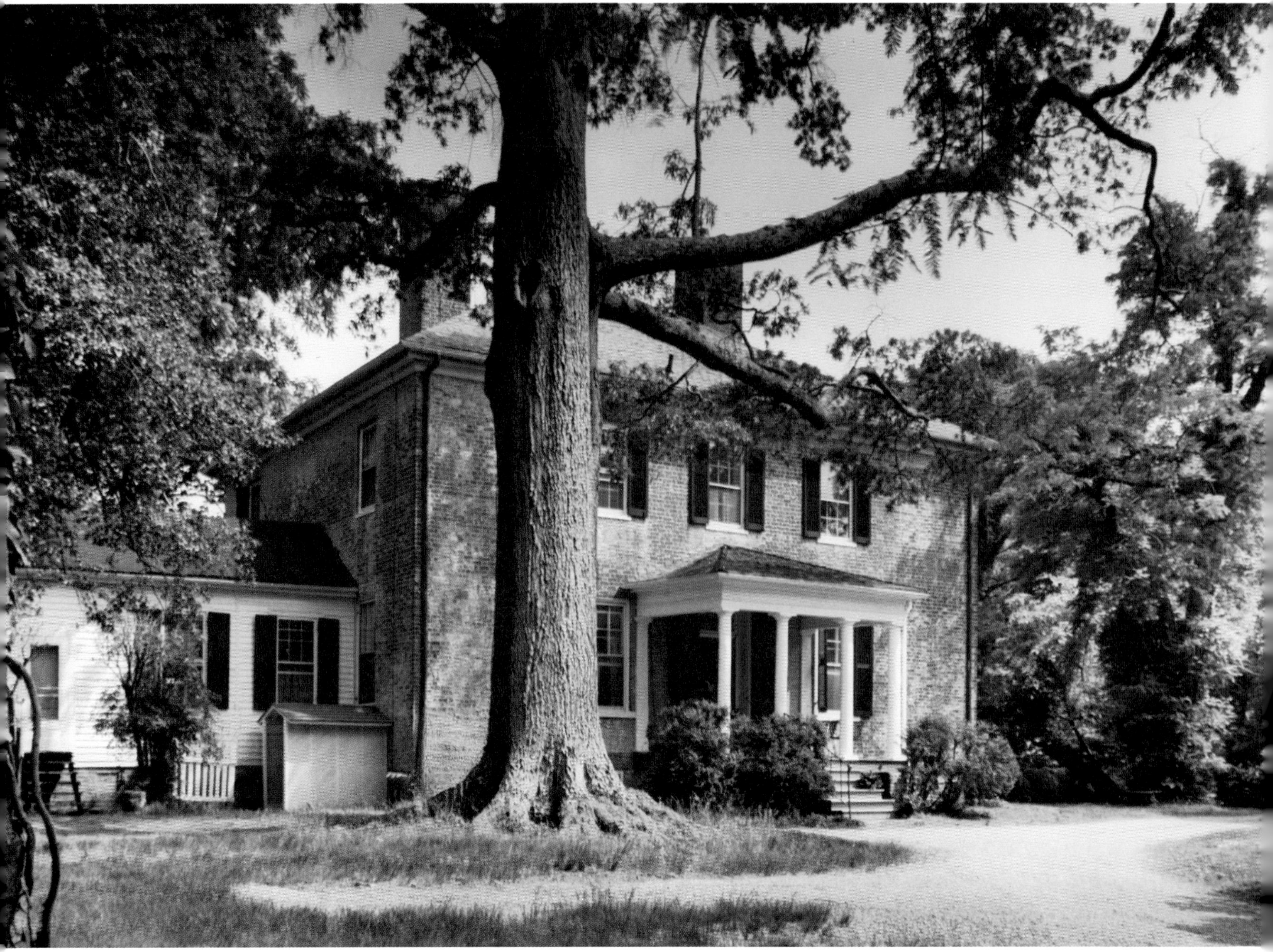

139 Fall Hill

An eighteenth century house on land thought to be part of Francis Thornton I's land patent of 1720, Fall Hill was remodelled about 1830. From the porch on the east side the town of Fredericksburg is visible year-round. The Fall Hill property was brought into the limits of the town in the 1984 annexation.

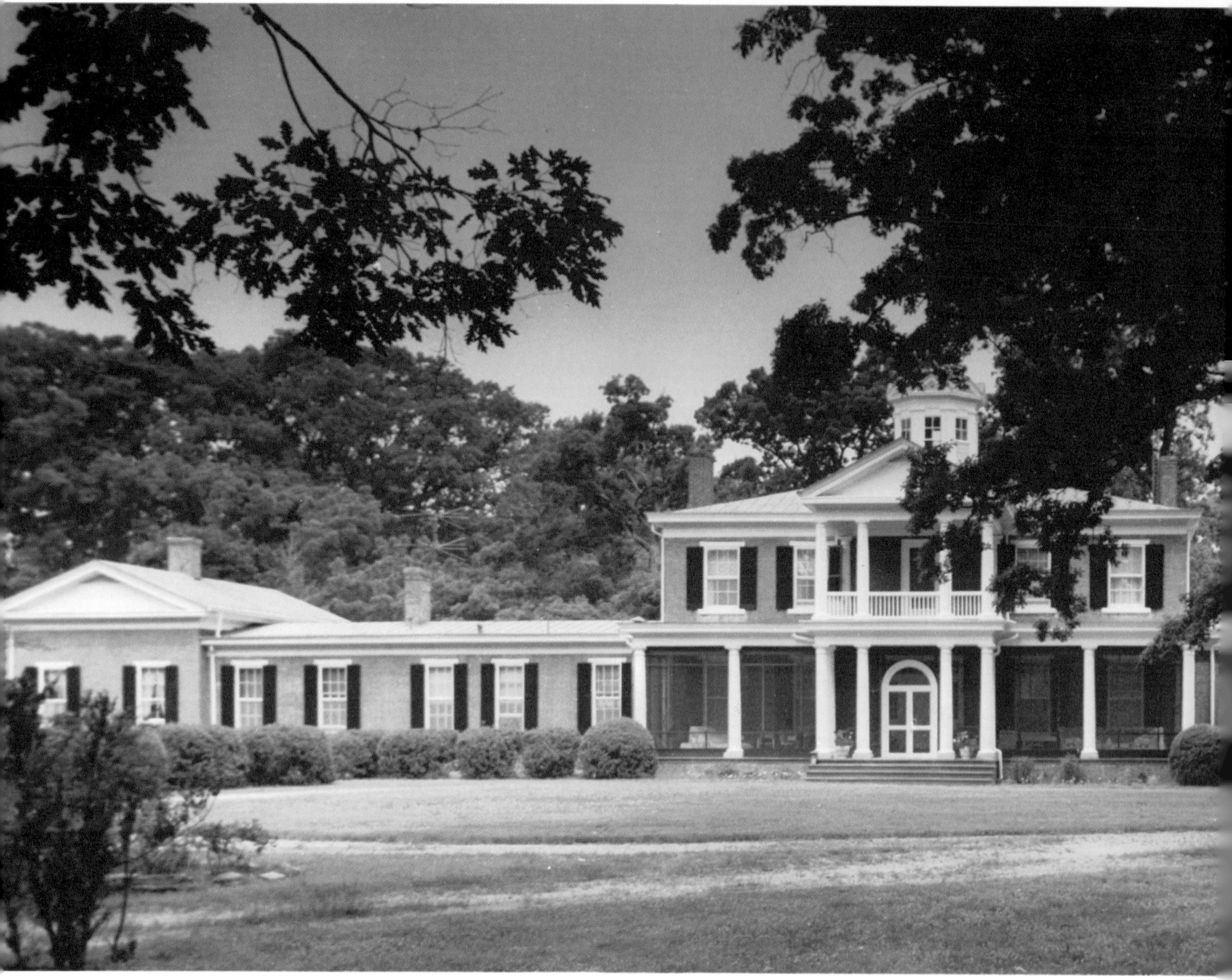

141 **Moss Neck Manor**

In nearby Caroline County is Moss Neck Manor, a pre-Civil War home built by James Corbin.

142 A sweeping view of the landscaped grounds from the second floor of the handsome collonaded porch. Moss Neck Manor is located in a predominately rural area east of Fredericksburg off the old main road to Port Royal and Tappahannock.

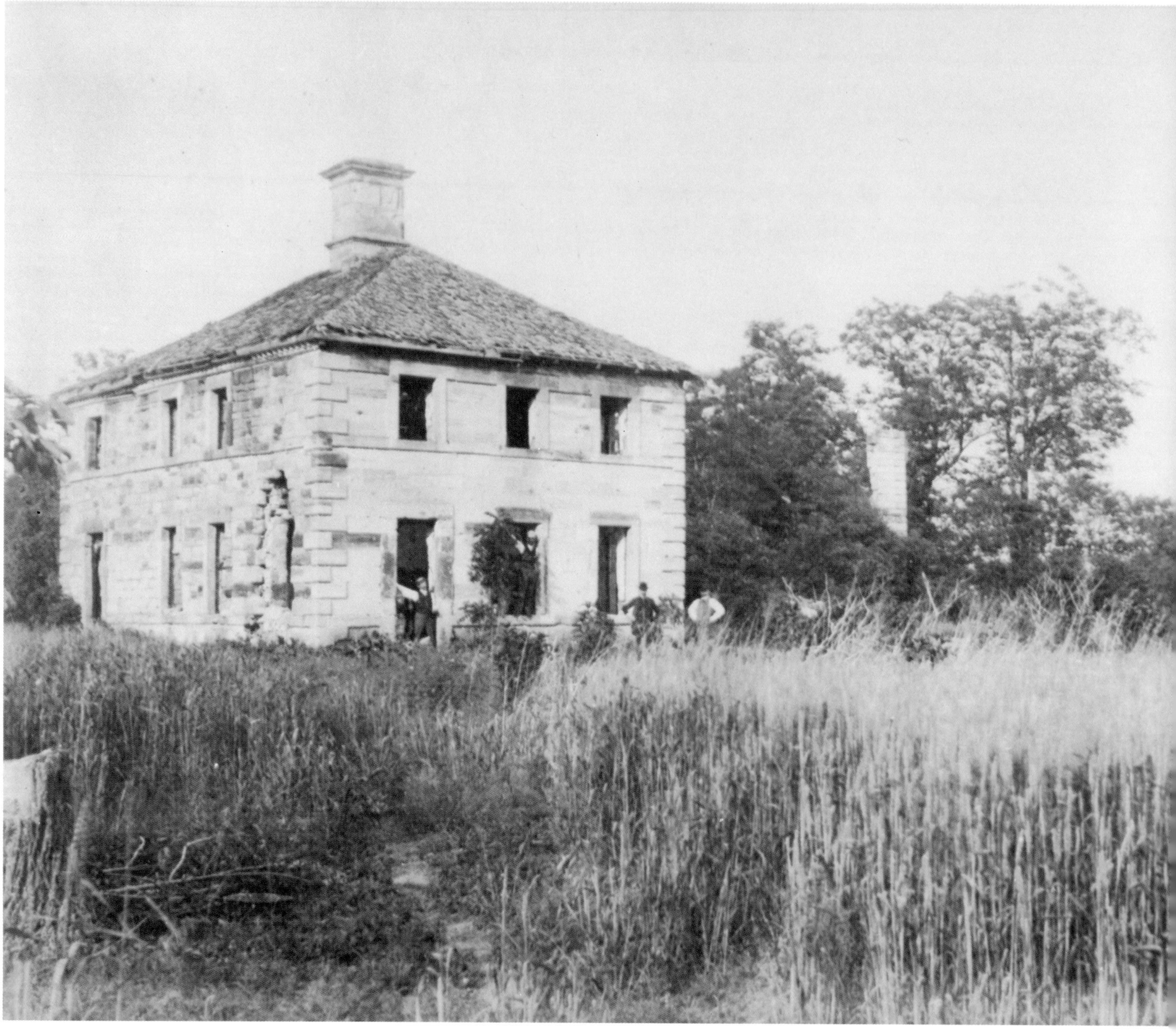

143 **Barnard House**

One of the finest houses in the Fredericksburg area, on the site now occupied by the Fredericksburg Country Club, Barnard House was a casualty of the battle of Fredericksburg. The house remained standing for many years after the war then collapsed. It is seen here about 1885.

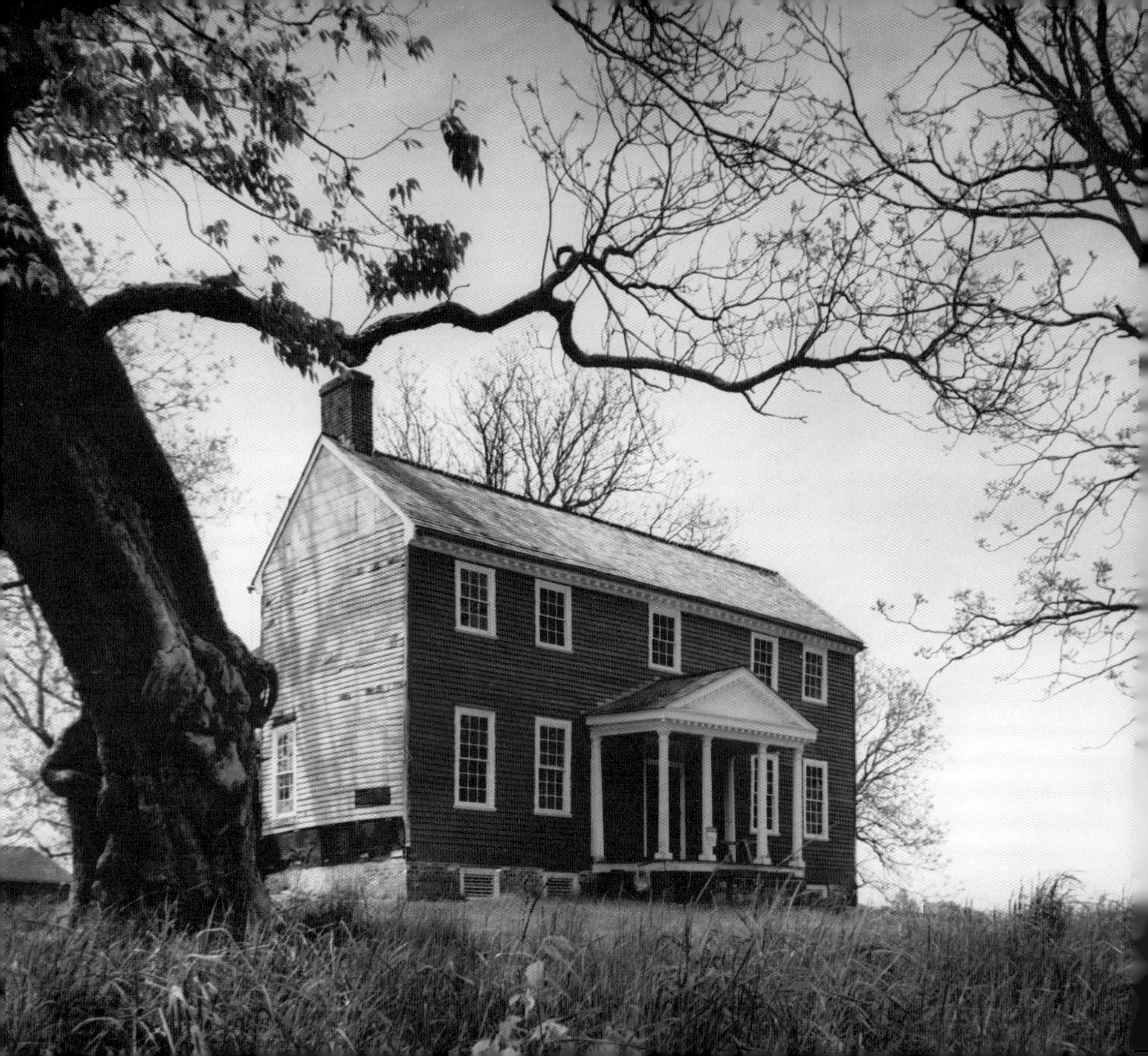

144 Ellwood on Wilderness Run

Erected by William Jones about 1795, Ellwood was drawn into the war during the fighting at Wilderness. Occupying a prominent hilltop site above Wilderness Run, Ellwood was an important observation point from which to observe the disposition of the armies below. An old photograph taken on the steps of the porch about 1900 reveals the Victorian era revisions made to the property. In the photograph are Robert C. Duvall and his family who farmed the land at the turn of the century.

Library of Congress

147 Oakley

Two views of Oakley, a Spotsylvania County plantation house built in 1817 by Samuel Alsop. The house appears now much as it did in 1927 when photographed by Frances Benjamin Johnston.

148 **Wilderness Baptist Church**

The most recent of several churches on or near this site near Wilderness Run west of Fredericksburg is this c. 1899 sanctuary of the Wilderness Baptist Church. The church site was in the path of both armies during the battles of Chancellorsville and Wilderness.

149 **Jackson Shrine**

General Thomas "Stonewall" Jackson, Robert E. Lee's most trusted subordinate, died in this small frame office in Guinea Station on May 10, 1863. Accidentally wounded by his own men at Chancellorsville on the night of May 2, Jackson was taken to the plantation of T. C. Chandler in Caroline County behind Confederate lines and near by main rail line to Richmond. Jackson's wound was complicated by pneumonia. The house has been restored by the National Park Service and is open to the public.

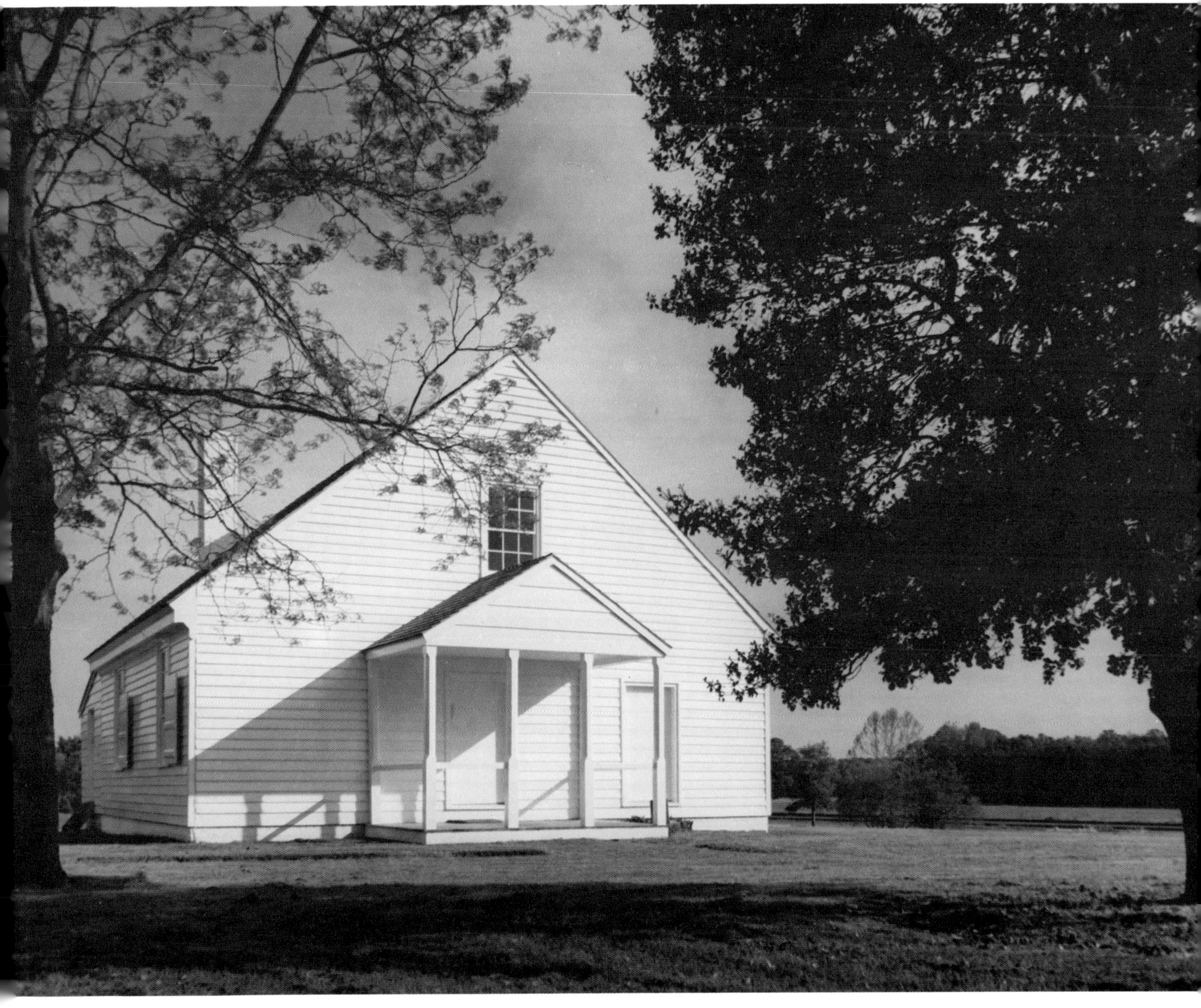

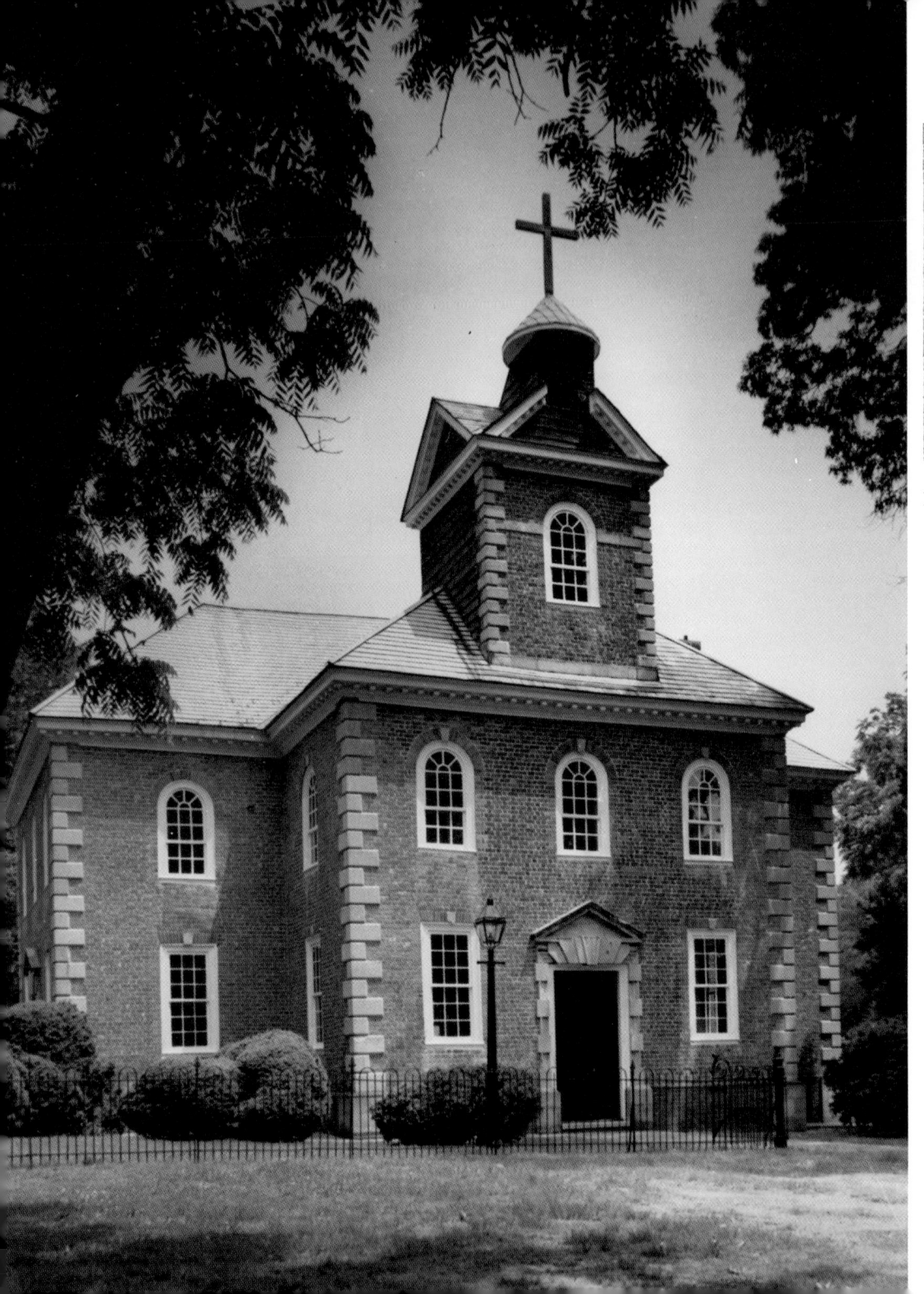

151 Aquia Church

The Episcopal church at Aquia (1751) is often called one of the best preserved colonial churches in Virginia. Among the many distinctive architectural features are the carved stone quoins at the entrances.

152 Restoration at Hartwood

The old manor house at Hartwood is being restored following years of neglect and a narrow escape from demolition by the Virginia Department of Highways. Built in 1826 by William Irving, an Irish immigrant, the house was the center of a 5,000 acre estate. It occupies a hillside site on Route 17, the road to Fredericksburg, about ten miles west of Falmouth.

152

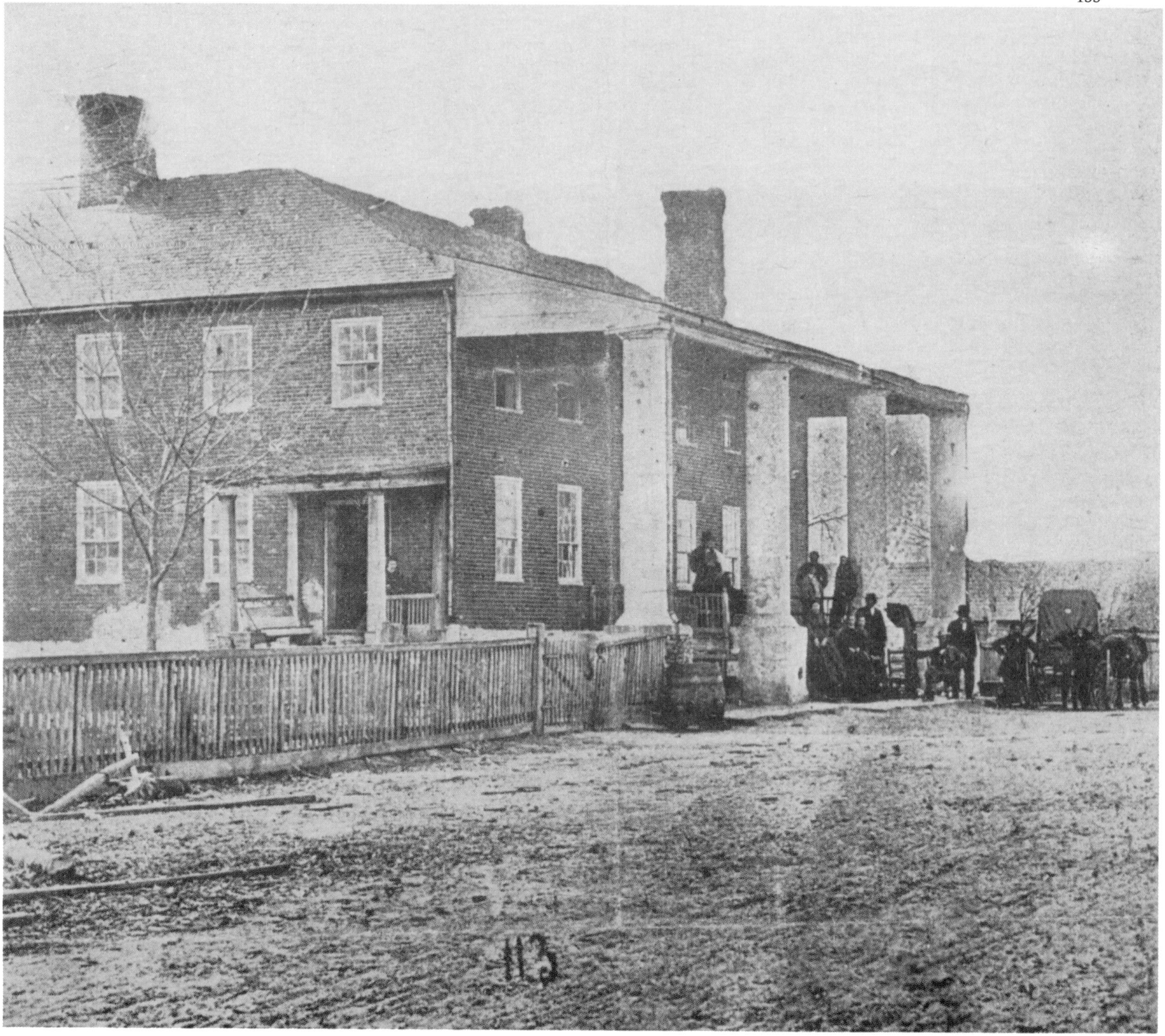

Library of Congress

153 The Hotel at Spotsylvania Court House, during the Civil War

154 **Pontoon Crossing from Chatham**

A private residence built in the 1930s occupies a site near the upper pontoon crossing used by Federal soldiers in 1862. The view is from the hill in front of Chatham.

134